Signs and Wonders in

ZIMBABWE

Beryl Shaw

Signs And Wonders In Zimbabwe by Beryl Shaw
Copyright © 2014 by Beryl Shaw
All Rights Reserved.
ISBN: 978-1-59755-370-4
Published by: ADVANTAGE BOOKS™
              Longwood, Florida USA
              www.advbookstore.com

Unless otherwise indicated, Bible quotations are taken from The Open Bible, New American Standard version. Copyright 1976 by Thomas Nelson Publishers.

Some names, marked with an asterisk (*), have been changed to protect identities.

Library of Congress Catalog Card Number: 2014946115

Cover Deisign by Pat Theriault

First Printing: September 2014
14 15 16 17 18 19 20   10 9 8 7 6 5 4 3 2 1
Printed in the United States of America

ACKNOWLEDGEMENTS

My sincere thanks go to my faithful husband, Mervyn, for his continued support, encouragement and assistance in so many ways. I feel that this writing is really a joint effort, and I am most grateful for Mervyn's input and contribution throughout the writing. We have walked this road together with God's help and in His strength.

I would also like to extend my sincere thanks to Ken with www.Book-Editing-Service.com for editing the manuscript and for his meaningful words of encouragement. My thanks also go to those who have offered helpful and critical suggestions, which have enabled me to relate experiences correctly. I would also like to extend my sincere thanks to my trustworthy friend Sue Goode for writing the foreword and to those who have contributed their personal testimonies.

To all my dear family and friends I say "Thank you" for your love, support and faithful prayers over so many years. Your encouragement and prayers have made this book possible.

I praise Almighty God for His constant faithfulness, protection and guidance throughout the years. His mercies never fail.

To Him be all the glory.
Beryl Shaw.

Beryl Shaw

TABLE OF CONTENTS

A NOTE FROM THE AUTHOR

I am always excited when relating miraculous happenings that took place during my 44 years in Zimbabwe.

One hears so many negative reports about what is happening in the country, but very rarely of the good and positive things. No matter how dark a situation God is always present and moving among His people in spectacular ways. His light shines brighter in the darkness, causing His name to be uplifted and glorified to a greater degree. I have a desire to share what I have witnessed and because of this have been prompted to write the following accounts as I recall them.

I was born in the county of Essex, in England, and emigrated to Rhodesia in 1960. I met Mervyn soon after my arrival in the country and we were married in Salisbury, the capital city, a year and a half later in 1962.

Mervyn and I were blessed with four children, first a daughter, Karen, then three sons, Kevin, Gregory and Craig respectively. All of the children were born in Salisbury between the years of 1967 and 1974.

Tension between the U.K. and Rhodesia had been growing in the country for some years and in 1965 the Prime Minister, Mr. Ian Smith, declared independence from Britain by a Unilateral Declaration. Britain responded by imposing sanctions upon Rhodesia and the first memory I have is that of fuel rationing. So began the start of the 17-year struggle of the war of independence, during which time the name of the country changed from Rhodesia to Zimbabwe Rhodesia, and finally to its existing name of Zimbabwe.

All four of our children were born within these years, and, as a result, had never known times of peace and ease. The foundation of their growing years was built on prayer; prayer for their every day needs, food, clothing, fuel, safety, school and medical needs, resulting in a strong faith and belief in the power of prayer.

Private medical insurance coverage was available for the public, but assistance through a benefit scheme was not part of the Rhodesian lifestyle. People were responsible for their own well-being and consequently employment was of paramount importance. Irresponsibility towards one's self or family commitments simply resulted in the distressful situation of a "no work, no pay" scenario. However, the positive effect of this lifestyle instilled in people a sense of responsibility and self-worth.

Although it has not been easy living in a war-torn land, watching a beautiful, self-supporting country with a stable lifestyle disintegrate; it has nevertheless been a privilege to share in the joys and sorrows of a courageous people, and to witness the power of Almighty God. To experience the tangibility of His supernatural power is far beyond the riches of silver and gold.

The following accounts have been written exactly as we experienced them. I have endeavoured to verify details to the best of my ability, but I may have made slight mistakes in the exact year in which particular events took place.

Many other accounts of God's supernatural interventions and healings have been written by both Rhodesians and Zimbabweans over the past three decades and I simply add my experiences to them, with the prayer that the Lord will use them for His glory.

Beryl Shaw.

"And these signs will accompany those who have believed; in My name they will cast out demons, they will speak with new tongues; they will pick up serpents, and if they drink any deadly poison, it shall not hurt them; they will lay hands on the sick, and they will recover." Mark 16: 17, 18.

FOREWORD

As I relive many of the miraculous works of God in this book, which I personally can vouch for, I truly rejoice that others will be able to know how we were sustained in perilous times.

Looking back at the testimonies of the different people recorded in this book, it becomes evident that our God is able to meet each individual at their point of need. It is my prayer that all who read of the variety of events in people's lives and the incredible answers to prayer, that each may be encouraged to put their trust in God.

It has been, and still is, a great blessing to call Beryl Shaw my friend. We have shared good times and hard times, but we were always able to look to Jesus, who in His great mercy and love answered our prayers.

May you who read this book give God the glory.

Sue (Goode.)

CHAPTER ONE

Clouds are Looming

"I will never desert you, nor will I ever forsake you."
Hebrews 13: 5b

Shortly after the declaration of independence, we seriously wondered if we were going to be subjected to an air attack by Britain as a Royal Air Force (RAF) squadron had been deployed to Zambia (a country bordering Rhodesia); but to our relief, this did not happen. Life continued on much the same as it had in previous years, except that fuel rationing was imposed. We had always had access to unlimited fuel, and with the blessing of a warm, sunny climate, would take advantage of the weekends to go off camping somewhere at a moment's notice. With the introduction of fuel rationing, however, our lifestyle immediately underwent radical change and these journeys had to cease. To keep within the limits of our ration, we made a concerted effort to reduce unnecessary journeys anywhere.

At this time Mervyn was employed as a firefighter with the Royal Rhodesian Air Force. We were stationed at the Thornhill Air Base in Gwelo and initially lived in a private free-standing house on an acre of ground, situated some two miles from the base. We loved this home, (even though it was positioned at the end of the runway, which took some getting used to as the planes flew directly over us). We were sorry when we had to move into the married quarters. Mervyn no longer needed transport for work as the quarters were stationed near the air base; whereas, I worked in the town of Gwelo a few miles away. Public transport was unavailable, so it was necessary for people commuting to work in the town to use their own transport. I soon joined up with three other ladies who worked in the town and we formed our own lift club. It was convenient that we all worked the same hours and the club ran well for a considerable length of time.

As our parents lived in Salisbury some 150 miles away, we endeavoured to save as much fuel as possible in an effort to visit them on occasions. These visits began to take on new meaning because we could no longer take any journeys for granted.

As time progressed we became slowly aware that certain foods and commodities were no longer available in the stores. Dried fruit and other such luxuries disappeared from supermarket shelves; cereals also became scarce. Many foods and other essential items had previously been imported from Britain and these were simply no longer available. And then a wonderful thing started to happen. Rhodesians started rising to the challenge and began producing a wide variety of goods themselves.

We well remember the first cereals produced! Honey Crunchies they were called. Initially they were *so sweet* that we could hardly bear to eat them! Much trial-and- error took place in those early years of sanctions, but little by little the country became far more self-supporting. I remember being puzzled by the fact that I could not buy clothes pegs anywhere. We then discovered that the small metal spring in the centre of the peg had actually been an imported product and these were no longer available. It did not take long before the steel works started producing the springs.

I share these first years of sanctions with the reader to give a background of how the Lord was dealing with His people, enabling them to become resilient in the face of hardship, and how, over a period of time, He very slowly drew them to Himself.

As sanctions continued people adjusted to the changes; fuel coupons became a way of life and imported luxury items such as dried and tinned fruit, sweets and chocolate gave way to a plainer diet. As time progressed the country learnt to produce a large variety of foodstuffs and other commodities which resulted in the country being far more self-supporting. During these early years the bush war, which had now commenced, did not affect those of us living in cities and urban areas.

Life continued on relatively peacefully and we were unaware of the lives that were being subjected to violence and other hardships in the bush and rural areas.

During the course of 1966, when I was expecting our first child, we received the very sad news that Mervyn's father had passed away very suddenly. We immediately drove to Salisbury, to be with my mother-in-law. However, on the strength of this sad and unexpected change in our lives, Mervyn was granted a posting (on compassionate grounds) to Salisbury to be closer to his mother. He was based at the New Sarum Air Force base a few miles from the city centre. We were pleased to be back in Salisbury and enjoyed visiting other members of our family.

At the beginning of January 1967, we were pleased to announce the safe arrival of our daughter Karen; and at the end of 1969, Kevin, our second child, was born. I had only just returned from the maternity home when Mervyn shared the news that he had received a transfer back to Gwelo. The news came as a shock to me and neither of us wanted to leave Salisbury. And so it was with sadness that we once again packed up and left our families.

The year that followed in Gwelo differed for us as a family from previous years. I was no longer working and had my hands full with running a large home and garden, besides looking after two young children. In an effort to avoid the extreme heat of the day and be ready for the children's early morning needs I would be up by 5 a.m., and have the house swept and polished daily by 6 a.m. Thereafter, the day passed by in a whirl of activity as I saw to the needs of home and family.

During the next year Mervyn had the opportunity to undergo a two-week parachute training course, which was to be held at New Sarum in Salisbury. A vacancy for a Parachute Jumping Instructor had come up, and an opportunity to re-muster was offered to all serving members. About a dozen applicants were interviewed and Mervyn, along with one other person, were selected to go forward for training and assessment. From Thornhill he was flown up to New Sarum, and for the duration of the course stayed in the sergeant's mess. Although extremely vigorous, and at times quite intensive, Mervyn enjoyed the challenge and exhilaration of all that it entailed, and also welcomed the opportunity of the training. For a number of years parachuting was something he had wanted to do. However, although he successfully completed the course, it was with great disappointment that a health problem prevented him from qualifying as an instructor and the other man secured the position.

At a later stage in the same year Mervyn received a temporary posting to New Sarum, where he was to take command of the Fire Section for three weeks while the person in charge was on leave. On a previous visit to Salisbury we had viewed a collapsible caravan (trailer tent) with a view to purchase. On the strength of this the children and I accompanied Mervyn to Salisbury, and prior to the commencement of his work, we purchased the caravan and towed it to the camping ground, some six miles from the city. While Mervyn was at work during the day I stayed in the camping ground with the children. The arrangement worked very well, as I enjoyed the freedom of the open air and the interaction with other campers. We looked forward to Mervyn's return at the end of the day and enjoyed evening walks around the spacious grounds. That year has always held particular significance for me, as one day while pushing the pram around the camping ground I vividly remember hearing an announcement on the radio to the effect that men had landed on the moon! This was certainly the hot topic of conversation in the ablution block that day! Eventually the three weeks came to an end; we happily towed the caravan back to our home in Thornhill and parked it in the back garden. We settled back into our daily routine, but now as time progressed we were becoming increasingly aware of impending danger closer to home.

By this time the bush war had intensified. Thousands of insurgents were entering the country through our unguarded borders. They were causing great disruption and terrorising the local populace in an effort to overthrow the government. Hundreds of men from within the country were being called up to serve in the army and air force to defend the land. Despair and despondency came upon those who received the devastating news that their loved ones had been killed in action. The reality of the seriousness of the situation came home to us when the young son of personal friends was killed. Families were being torn apart and the stability of the country was being seriously threatened. Time and time again our hopes lifted as government officials visited from Britain to negotiate peace talks with the Prime Minister. Sadly, it was to no avail. The war continued and simply exacerbated.

Further change occurred in our lives when, during 1970, the country decimalised and all units of measurement changed to the metric system. Initially, for many people, it was difficult to adjust to the new system, but, as with everything else taking place in around us, it soon became a new way of life.

CHAPTER TWO

Adjusting to Change

"The eternal God is a dwelling place, and underneath are the everlasting arms." Deuteronomy 33:27a

Towards the end of 1969, following lengthy discussions between us, Mervyn made the decision to leave the air force and return to civilian life. So, at the end of January 1970, with the caravan in tow, we drove out of the married quarters for the last time and returned to our home in Salisbury. Once again, it was good to be closer to our family and we soon adjusted to civilian life.

A few years later after our third child, Gregory, had been born, we decided to visit some friends in the Lowveld, some 160 kilometres from Salisbury. John* and Susan* had bought the Elephant Hills Motel which was situated on the main road, approximately 100 kilometres from the border post between Rhodesia and South Africa.

Due to the unrest and danger in the country, protection was now given to civilians travelling in remote areas and convoys were provided along certain routes. We were very keen to visit our friends, but it was with some trepidation that we travelled 150 kilometres in a convoy of approximately 20 cars. Armoured vehicles were positioned at the front and the back of the convoy as we made our way along the dangerous route. The children were instructed to get down on to the floor in the event of any gunfire. Eventually, with great relief and no incidents, we safely arrived at our destination and were happy to meet up with our friends.

The three days we spent with John, Susan and their young children were most enjoyable, and we marvelled at their resilience and courage living in such a remote place. John was a paraplegic, so negotiating in a wheelchair through the stony, uneven pathways surrounding the hotel was no mean feat, but he was always up for a challenge and they were a very enterprising couple.

The evening before our departure a new development raised great concern. Reports had come in to the effect that shooting had broken out very close to the hotel and we had to give serious thought to our departure the following morning. However, later in the evening a policeman arrived and assured us that the situation had been brought under control. As it was necessary for Mervyn to return to work we decided to go ahead and leave early the following morning, which we duly did. Once again we travelled in convoy without incident and later that day arrived back at our home safely.

Our fourth and last child, Craig, was born in 1974. My mother had died from cancer when he was 18 months old, and my elder brother died in a car accident a year and a half later. Due to the unsettled situation in the country thousands of people were leaving every month, including over a period of time, all the members of my family. One of my younger brothers had been serving in the air force for several years and had narrowly escaped death on several occasions. He left with his wife and three young children.

By this time Mervyn had joined the Volunteer Reserves in the Air Force and for a number of years he alternated between six weeks at home and six weeks in the bush. Initially this was hard to accept and, for the family, every time of parting was difficult. As with all other families our men folk were committed to prayer daily.

Another serious threat to our peace and stability occurred in December 1978 when the country's fuel supply, which was stored in a number of massive metal tanks less than a mile from the city centre, was set alight as a result of a rocket attack. It was blazing furiously.

Many people were praying as men at the fuel depot worked tirelessly to drain off the fuel and to bring the inferno under control. The potential loss to the country could hardly be calculated as almost all vehicular transport would have been halted; and in a country that was already undergoing fuel rationing, people were threatened by the fear of our stocks being exhausted. However, the Lord encouraged us through His word and gave us His promise from 1 Kings 17: 14, "For thus says the Lord God of Israel, 'The bowl of flour shall not be exhausted, nor shall the jar of oil be empty, until the day that the Lord sends rain on the face of the earth.'"

Eventually, after a number of days, the inferno was brought under control and extinguished. The bravery of the fire-fighters and workers from the fuel depot was admired by all. Miraculously no one was hurt or injured and hundreds of Christians gave thanks to almighty God for His amazing intervention.

On two occasions bombs went off in the city, but once again, incredibly, there were no casualties. Even newspaper coverage of the second incident drew attention to the fact that "only one sparrow had been killed."

Obviously throughout the years we experienced the good and the bad times, but no matter what the day brought we were aware of God's presence with us. Day in and day out He continued to strengthen and encourage His people. Even in the darkest times He revealed Himself in wondrous and supernatural ways, continually reminding us of His promise from 1 Corinthians 10:13, "No temptation has overtaken you but such as is common to man; and God is faithful, who will not allow you to be tempted beyond what you are able, but with the temptation will provide the way of escape also, that you may be able to endure it."

One afternoon, as I was working in the lounge, I was suddenly taken by surprise when our friend Shirley came rushing in through the open French doors. She was in a very distressed state. Hurrying straight across to our radio she switched it on, asking me at the same time if I'd heard the news, to which I replied "that I had not." We listened together in horror to the report of a Viscount passenger plane having been shot down in the north of the country by a hand-held missile launcher. The news of the disaster was quite bad enough, but I was even more shocked to learn that a close friend of Shirley's, who had just got married and was on her honeymoon, had been on the plane.

The whole country was in shock, a bush war was one thing, but to shoot down a civilian plane was beyond the understanding of ordinary men and women. There had been survivors and at a later stage we met the last remaining man. He had survived the initial crash, along with others, into the harsh sun-baked bush land, and had gone in search of water. However, on his return he was devastated to discover that the remaining survivors had been massacred.

At a later stage a second Viscount passenger plane was also shot down by a hand-held missile launcher, but on this occasion the insurgents did not massacre the survivors.

The city of Umtali is situated approximately 15 kilometres from the border of Mozambique. Insurgents were continually coming in to the country and terrorising the lives of the inhabitants. Incredibly, throughout the duration of the war, only two bombs were fired at the city. One missed its target, flying over a building and landing in vacant ground beyond. The second landed in a small shop causing much damage, yet the owner walked out of the store unharmed! It was reported that, no matter the season, a cloud in the form of a hand hung over the city of Umtali from one year until the next. The residents believed that this was God's tangible sign of protection and claimed Isaiah 51:16 as His promise to them.

"And I have put My words in your mouth, and have covered you with the shadow of My hand, to establish the heavens, to found the earth, and to say to Zion, 'You are My people.' "

Indeed, over the years the reports of God's protection upon the inhabitants of Umtali were nothing short of miraculous. We have been privileged to hear the testimonies of people living there, and to read accounts that have been published.

In 1977, soon after Mervyn and I became Christians, we started praying about how we could serve the Lord together. I was, shortly after, invited to attend a church conference, which was to be held at the Salisbury University. At the end of one evening session I went forward for prayer. A visiting speaker, from South Africa, prayed for me and said, "The Lord is calling you into a new service for Him, and He will equip you." I was quite amazed, and returned to my chair. As I sat down a young man, a member of the youth group, leaned across to me and said, "Mrs. Shaw, I believe the Lord is calling you and Mr. Shaw to be the new youth group leaders." I was even more amazed. I returned home, and shared this with Mervyn.

We were quite in favour of this idea, and started to pray about this specific area. Our main concern was that we had four young children and we were not very happy about the idea of having them out late every week. Then, one morning, in my Bible reading the question was asked, "How could you use your home for the Lord?" and I knew immediately that the Lord was directing us to hold the youth meetings in our home. We had a large lounge, and could easily accommodate the group. I suggested this to Mervyn, and he was in agreement with the idea. We then felt that we just had to wait and pray. About two weeks later we were enjoying a day's outing with the youth at Cleveland Dam, a reservoir on the outskirts of the city. Rev. Rob and Shirley Corder were leading the group at that time. Rob called Mervyn and me aside and asked us if we would pray about the possibility of committing ourselves to the leadership of the youth group. We laughed, and told him that we had no need to pray because we had already had it confirmed by the Lord. Rob had actually known for about six weeks, but had been waiting for the Lord's perfect timing before approaching us. Both Rob and Shirley were in agreement about the use of our home, even though they had young children of their own. We were most grateful. Under their excellent leadership, Mervyn and I underwent four years of intense training. It was not easy for us, as we had never been involved in anything like this before, and we had much to learn. The four years comprised meetings, camps, conferences, and one "never to be forgotten" retreat in a local home, during which time the Lord moved in miraculous ways.

One evening about 20 people were gathered in our home for a youth meeting. We had just spent time in praise and worship and had gone to prayer when the telephone rang. A prayer request for protection for the city of Umtali came through. Two thousand insurgents, supported by Russian made tanks, had gathered on the borders and were planning to invade the city that night. We immediately went to prayer, asking the Lord to intervene and avert the situation. It was wonderful to know that our prayers were linked with hundreds of other Christians across the land, all praying in one accord. We were thrilled to learn the following morning that during the course of the night the enemy forces, for "no apparent reason," had dispersed and returned to their own country. We had much to thank and praise the Lord for.

It was never a surprise to receive outside call for prayer coverage, and, once again we were gathered in our home for a youth meeting when a second prayer request came through for protection for the residents of Umtali. Once again the situation was taken to the Lord and we prayed earnestly to Him, asking Him to defuse the impending attack. We learnt later that bombs had been launched at the city's main hotel, but had failed to detonate. Also, a vehicle carrying a large amount of arms had been captured intact in the city centre and no one had been injured.

As two senior members of the youth group had been called up to serve in the forces, they were kept continually in our prayers. They were serving in very dangerous areas, "hotspots" as they were known. One young man was riding "shotgun" on the front of trains as they travelled through miles of bush land, sometimes open ground and at other times heavily wooded. These areas were renowned for insurgent activity, but, praise God, at the end of his call up he returned to us unscathed.

Another member of the group had some very close encounters with death. Some of his colleagues lost their lives right beside him, and on one occasion he was in a vehicle that hit a landmine. Praise the Lord, this young man was miraculously saved in this particular incident, although his hearing was affected as a result of the explosion. We felt it time to pray him out of active service, and this prayer was soon answered in the form of a transfer to a desk job.

CHAPTER THREE

The Power of Prayer

"Again, I say to you, that if two of you agree on earth about anything that they may ask, it shall be done for them by my father who is in heaven. For where two or three have gathered together in my name, there I am in their midst."
Matthew 18:19, 20.

Throughout the years I became involved in several weekly prayer groups, each one centering in on specific needs. One day I had met with several other mothers to pray for the safety of the school children. Various safety precautions had been put in place in the schools, including named suitcases. All the children had their names written boldly on the outside of their case for immediate identification. They were also taught bomb drills in the event of attack. At the first sign of danger the children had to climb underneath their desks. We impressed upon the children the need for prayer and praise in this event. Amongst other needs, many of them travelled considerable distances by bus through unsettled areas. There was no doubt that the Lord had laid a specific burden on our hearts on this particular day. It was therefore with great amazement later in the day that we learnt of His intervention and protection.

At one point along the route there was an unmanned level crossing on the main road. Although road signs were in position warning of the danger, there were no warning lights or booms to prevent vehicles from going through. The school bus was travelling slowly as it approached the crossing. On either side of the railway tracks tall mealies (maize) plants were growing, which obscured the driver's view. As a result he failed to see an approaching train and continued on towards the crossing. As the train crossed the road the bus collided with the side of the train, but it miraculously bounced back a few metres. Apart from shock, there were no injuries and we praised the Lord for His protection upon all of the passengers in the bus.

Another group I became involved with was named "Operation Esther." (I believe the name is self-explanatory.) This group was raised up specifically to pray for the farmers and their families, who, by this time, were undergoing fierce attacks upon themselves and their properties. After taking the children to school I would drive in to the city, a distance of approximately 10 kilometres and there meet up with approximately 60 or 70 other ladies. They came from many areas surrounding the city and it was encouraging and uplifting to be part of this committed, vibrant group. The meeting commenced with prayer followed by a speaker, who encouraged and inspired us to continue on faithfully in prayer. Many reports of God's miraculous protection and intervention in the lives of the farmers and their families were brought to us.

Following the speaker, we would then split up into small groups and spend the next hour in prayer. Each of us was furnished with the names and areas of specific families for whom we were to pray, not only in these meetings, but on a daily basis.

A number of years later it was wonderful to read of research that had taken place. It had been possible to link up specific times of protection of people, or interventions in times of danger, with exact times that intercessors were praying for the families.

I share with you some of the accounts that were verified.

One evening an elderly couple living on their own in a remote farmhouse were on their knees in prayer. They knew that their home was surrounded by insurgents and they were expecting an attack at any moment, but nothing happened. It was reported the following day that while the insurgents were preparing for an attack on the farmhouse, Rhodesian troops came across them and captured them. When asked why they had not opened fire on the farmhouse the response was, "We could not get a clear shot because of the soldiers in white surrounding the building!" Many other similar reports came back to us, one of which was a mother walking down the garden path with her two small children, unaware of imminent danger. Once again insurgents were caught and questioned and the reply was the same, "We could not get a clear shot at the people because of the soldiers in white walking with them!"

Another report was that of a farmer travelling on a dusty road in his Land Rover when a whirlwind suddenly sprang up before him. The dust was so thick and impaired his vision to such an extent that he was forced to stop. When the whirlwind passed, the farmer saw that the wind had uncovered a landmine approximately two metres in front of one of his front wheels!

These reports and many more that were verified continued to pour in, week by week and month by month. Attending the meetings was not always easy due to the unrest in the country. There were even times when, having dropped the children at school on my way to a meeting, I actually wondered whether I would safely return to see them again. However, the Lord remained faithful and He continued to protect and encourage us. In one of the meetings, during the singing of the hymn *Onward Christian Soldiers* (Arthur Seymour Sullivan 1842-1900), I was reminded that we were not only in a physical war, but a spiritual one also. *"For our struggle is not against flesh and blood, but against the rulers, against the powers, against the spiritual forces of wickedness in the heavenly places."* (Ephesians 6:12.) Therefore, we would put on the armour of God, stand in His strength and continue to trust Him one day at a time.

Besides being involved with the prayer groups, I was also a member of a very busy prayer chain. During the course of the day many requests came through. The needs were many and varied and the prayer chain ran successfully for a number of years. Strict control and confidentiality were maintained at all times. Throughout the years we were greatly blessed and encouraged by the miraculous answers we received.

In the months and years that followed we were to learn how God delights to answer our prayers, often in the most amazing and startling ways. He called us to follow Him and trust Him, no matter what the circumstances. Little did I know what blessings lay ahead as a result of one simple phone call I received one day. The call was from a member of the youth group, Grant. He and his mother, Kath Walton, were planning to visit her elderly father, Mr. Healey, who lived in a remote valley towards Dombashawa. The trip was some 24 kilometres from Salisbury and I was invited to accompany them. I was very excited to receive the invitation because I had heard so much about this valley. On the day arranged we set off by car in the hot morning sun and travelled along the wide tarred roads that led through the city and out into the country. The miles of bush land opened up before us as we left the outskirts of the city.

The area was known to be dangerous, but this did not abate my excitement as we approached the valley. Eventually we left the tarred road and turned on to one of the many dirt roads which criss-crossed the country. At the start of the descent into the valley stood a welcoming sign, which read, "Resthaven." "Come ye apart and rest awhile." Resthaven, (also known as "Miracle Valley,") was the name given by the late Reverend Frank Mussell, who had been given the vision of building a number of cottages in the valley as a place where missionaries and church workers could go to rest and recuperate from their busy lifestyle. Mr. Healey, a man now in his 70s , was the last remaining resident in one of the cottages. He had been the caretaker at Resthaven for many years. As the area had become so dangerous the other residents had left. However, Mr. Healey refused to leave his beloved home.

As we drove in amongst the now vacant cottages, my heart was overwhelmed by the beauty of the indigenous Msasa trees and the peace that pervaded the area. While Kath visited her father, Grant and I walked around the area. The entire complex comprised approximately 15 cottages, a beautiful little chapel and a conference centre. I fell in love with the rustic cottages and the natural, unspoiled beauty of the area. A stream ran through the valley and a youth centre with an outdoor swimming pool had been built at the far end of the valley.

We would have loved to have visited the youth camp, but in view of the sensitive situation it was safer, and more sensible, not to venture farther. Instead, we climbed a short way up the side of a hill, and there, amongst the beautiful trees, we sat and gazed upon the peaceful scene surrounding us. If it were not for the shotgun laying beside Grant on that idyllic morning, we could almost have imagined that the country was at peace. As we sat and surveyed our surroundings, Grant suddenly verbalised my own unspoken thoughts, he said, "Wouldn't it be fantastic if we could bring the youth group here for a camp."

Under our present circumstances, the very thought of bringing a group of teenagers to a dangerous, unsettled area was out of the question. However, the longing in our hearts was so great that we prayed that the Lord would restore peace to the land, that He would open up the valley once again and make it possible for us to hold a youth camp there. Little did we know how the Lord was going to answer our prayers and shower us with His blessings in the years to come.

CHAPTER FOUR

Equipped for Service

*"And do not get drunk with wine, for that is dissipation, but be
filled with the Spirit, speaking to one another in psalms and
hymns and spiritual songs, singing and making melody with
your heart to the Lord." Ephesians 5:18, 19.*

The weekly youth meetings continued on in our home under the
leadership of Rob and Shirley. Shirley led the singing with her guitar, and
over the months some of the young people bought guitars and started
learning to play. After about two years I, too, felt that the Lord was
speaking to me about learning to play the instrument and so I committed
it to Him. In our circumstances funds were not available for luxuries such
as musical instruments, so I prayed and waited on the Lord. It was not
long after that I shared my thoughts with a friend, Irene and her
immediate response was one of joy and confirmation at the idea of me
learning to play. She shared with me that her daughter's guitar was at
home in the cupboard, and explained that it was not being used at this
time because her daughter was away at boarding school. Irene then went
on to say that "she would just love to lend it to me to learn on for the
Lord's service." I was quite astounded at this kind offer, but as we were
not in the habit of borrowing things I asked for time to think and pray
about it. My main concern was for the safety of the instrument, I was
afraid of taking responsibility for it lest it should become damaged.

It was at this time that I went into hospital for an operation, as I was to
have bunions removed from both feet. Just prior to the operation I had

been reading a book called "Nine O'Clock in the Morning." (Author Dennis J. Bennett, published by Bridge Logos Foundation, 1970; edited by John Sherill.) The story was based on Acts Chapter 2, which covers the coming of the Holy Spirit. As the Spirit moved upon me I became very excited about what I was reading. I decided to put the teaching to the test and find out if I had been given the gift of tongues. To my delight I simply spoke quietly to myself and, praise the Lord I was speaking in another language! By now I had been given a pre-med prior to the operation and the curtains had been drawn around me. As I lay excitedly praying, completely at peace over what lay ahead, I suddenly heard a gentle voice calling my name. I recognised the voice as that of a friend and called out in answer. To my delight she had brought me a gift of a book from the church Women's Association. I was thrilled to see her and was very grateful for the book.

Eventually I was taken to the theatre and underwent the operation. I remember coming around from the anaesthetic at approximately 6:30 p.m. I was aware of the intense pain in my feet and accepted a pain killer. I was also aware of being asked if I would like something to eat which I accepted, then declined when the meal arrived. I fell into a deep sleep and did not wake up until the next morning. To my sheer delight and amazement I discovered that I had no pain in my feet. The surgeon examined his work later that morning and was satisfied with the results. For myself I was thrilled with my "new look!" He then encouraged me to get up and walk in the afternoon. This I managed to do, slowly but with not too much discomfort. I learnt at a later stage, that at the exact time when I came around from the anaesthetic the previous evening, the choir had met for practice and had been praying for me.

I soon learnt that all the ladies in the ward with me were Christians. This was a double blessing and we had much to share. It goes without saying that I remained in my excited state and was eager to share my experience of the gift of tongues with Shirley, when she visited soon after the operation.

After I returned home it was necessary for me to put my feet up and rest as much as possible. This was not an easy thing for me to cope with as I was used to being very active. As I gave further thought to my friend's offer of the loan of the guitar I felt that I should now accept it, on the proviso that we pray and ask the Lord to provide me with a guitar of my own. I did not want to be responsible for the instrument for an indefinite period. Irene was in agreement and, having cleared the loan of the instrument with her daughter, she promptly brought it around to me. I immediately started to practice with a few chords that Shirley had given me. She had written them into a book of familiar praise songs, which was a good way to commence. Initially I thought that mastering the changes of the chords was quite beyond me. Having to stop singing midsentence, while I waited for my fingers to catch up with my voice, was utterly frustrating. If it had it not been for the fact that I was forced to rest and put my feet up, I do not think that I would ever had had the patience to persevere. There is no doubt that the Lord knew me through and through and His timing was ever perfect. Obviously I still needed exercise and at intervals I would walk around in my bandaged feet. On seeing a visitor, Grant, to the door on one occasion he said, "Mrs. Shaw, should you be walking around like that?" I replied that "I had not been told not to." In actual fact my feet healed very quickly and relatively painlessly, and within a week of being discharged I was able to attend the church services again.

Within a very short while the Lord answered our prayers for a guitar and we were informed of one being sold in our area for $15, an absolute "give-away." What was even more amazing was the fact that for the first time that we could remember, we actually had $15 left over from Mervyn's salary that month! We thanked and praised the Lord once again for His supply.

Although I continued to practice playing the guitar, it was many months before I actually had the courage to use it in the youth meetings. This did not come about until Rob and Shirley left Zimbabwe, at which time Mervyn and I took over the leadership of the group. I was then thrown in the deep end as somebody else had to lead!

During this time I was led to attend a "Life in the Spirit" seminar, which was being held at the convent in Salisbury. I had already met the lively nun who was conducting the seminar and the weekly meetings spent at the school were an absolute blessing to me. Sr. Marcia* was on fire for the Lord; her lifestyle exuded the love and joy of the Lord to such an extent that all those attending the seminar could not fail to experience life-changing encounters. For one of the sessions I was asked to take my guitar along and lead the singing. I was very nervous and, still being tied to my song book and chords, did not experience the same freedom in worship that I was used to when somebody else was leading. However, Sr. Marcia was most enthusiastic and encouraging; she prayed for me and asked the Lord to use me with my guitar in His service and for His glory in the years to come. This prayer was indeed answered in the years to come and in the most unexpected ways.

CHAPTER FIVE

Spiritual Growth

"But grow in the grace and knowledge of our Lord and Saviour Jesus Christ." 2 Peter 3:18a

After the youth group had been running for a while, thought was being given to the possibility of holding a camp over a long week-end. As suitable venues were not easily located, this became a priority for prayer. Excitement rose within the group when friends living locally offered their home for the purpose. The family was going away for that period and were happy for us to be on the premises, rather than leave the property vacant. The double-storied house was delightful, and most appropriate for our purpose. An added attraction was the outdoor swimming pool!

One morning while preparing for the camp, Shirley and I were seated in her lounge and giving thought to the catering. On my arrival at her home she explained that she had a doctor's appointment later that day for her eye, which was haemorrhaging. It didn't look good at all, but we kept on working. After some time Shirley turned to me and said, "This is awful. I can't see properly to work. Pray for my eye!" I placed my hand over her eye and asked the Lord to heal it. We then continued to work. A little while later I turned to her to say something, and what I saw made me gasp. She asked me what was wrong, and I simply said, "Oh, your eye." She put her hand to her eye and asked, "Why, what is wrong?" I explained that it had completely cleared and that there was no sign of haemorrhaging! We thanked and praised the Lord, and Shirley phoned and cancelled her appointment with the doctor. She had no more trouble with her eye.

I know that out of the two of us I was the most amazed at the wonderful answer to prayer. It certainly increased my faith, and served to strengthen my belief in a powerful God of healing.

Approximately 20 people, including young people and leaders with their families, attended the camp. The home was an ideal venue; the house was set amongst huge rocks on an acre of wooded ground. Between sessions, where time permitted, we had plenty of space to spend time alone. There was also a rustic hut built high above the ground, and accessed by a ladder. The secluded room was an ideal place for quiet prayer and meditation.

We truly praised the Lord for the way He provided and blessed us in so many different ways. Shirley and I managed the catering between us, preparing the main meals at home prior to the camp. As the local shops were within easy walking distance, we had no trouble in purchasing the odd grocery item when needed. The weather, as usual for Zimbabwe, was hot and sunny, ideal for the odd dip in the swimming pool. The youngest children, just a few years old, entertained themselves while sessions were taking place. As I look back I now I realize how the Lord had His hand of protection on the children. While we were involved indoors they happily spent their time scrambling over the rocks, (most of them three to four metres high. but some well over six metres) and climbing the trees which surrounded the house, and up the ladder to the hut! Praise the Lord the pool was fenced and gated!

Our week-end away at the youth camp was one of spiritual growth and healing in the lives of all who attended. Our times of worship drew us closer to the Lord and the in-depth teaching we received from Rob, especially relating to the work of the Holy Spirit in our lives, further equipped us for work in His service.

Emphasis on openness and honesty in relationships, though sometimes painful, strengthened bonds between us. It also opened the way for the Holy Spirit to move unhindered in our times of praise and worship, enabling us to experience a new freedom in the Lord. The presence of Almighty God was so tangible that there were occasions when people simply fell under His power. Lives were touched and changed, and they would never be the same again. Following the camp the young people became even more enthused to learn more about God, and their desire to follow Him wholly increased. There were even some within the group who would have preferred to have spent all of the weekly sessions in teaching, prayer and worship alone, but were told by the leadership "that they were still young and also needed lighter times of relaxation!" much to their disappointment.

It was encouraging to see the growth and enthusiasm of the young people, which extended beyond the weekly meetings. At one stage some of the senior members met for prayer daily, before school. They gathered together under a tree, just a short distance from our home, and brought their daily needs and concerns before the Lord. Their support of one another in this way was very rewarding, both for themselves and for us. The witness in the homes of these young people, (many from non-Christian backgrounds) was exemplary, and over the years the Lord used their submission and obedience to their parents to draw other family members into the Kingdom of God.

Tony, one of the senior members of the group, was a young man with a very cheerful character who lived life with great exuberance. His love of life, and light-hearted approach to things generally, was really quite infectious. People were drawn to him, they felt relaxed and at peace in his presence. A powerful memory I have of Tony was the depth of his implicit faith in the Lord with regards to the running of his car. The vehicle was a Mini, which Tony used to use to transport the youngsters in to meetings. As with most people at that time, funds were limited, and Tony was never in a position to put more than a few dollars worth of fuel into the tank at any one time. It never ceased to amaze us how the fuel gauge was always on the "empty" mark, yet the car never ran out of fuel; it always made it to its destination. The number of passengers that Tony actually managed to squeeze into the vehicle at any one time was also beyond comprehension!

Also within the youth group was a young woman by the name of Elsie. Tony and Elsie became good friends and in later years married. In 1982 they moved to South Africa and eventually settled in the small town of Stanger, where they soon became involved with the life and work of the church. It was here that the first of their children were born. The couple were very well-suited and had a great love for children. In recent years I have learnt that they eventually had a family of 10 children, five boys and five girls. We are thrilled to say that Tony and Elsie (as with the majority of the young people who attended the youth group), remained strong in their faith and have grown up serving the Lord, not only in Zimbabwe, but in also other countries as the Lord has sent them out.

For Tony and Elsie, praise and worship is central to their lives and within these first years Tony, along with another vibrant member of the church, was used in leading the worship in the services. The church grew tremendously and many miracles were witnessed. It was an exciting time for the family and precious friendships were made during these initial years. In later years they moved to Phalaborwa where they were used in ministry in building a church, which Tony pastored for a number of years. Again, they found the work both challenging and exciting. During these years their third and fourth children were born.

Throughout the years Tony and Elsie's home was constantly open to people of all ages; it was a place of warmth, love and healing to many people over the years. Apart from the care of their own growing family, other children were taken care of or fostered, and their numbers in the home were constantly fluctuating. In 1999, they began to home school their children and word of this new venture soon spread. It was not long before other people approached them, requesting that their children were taken in for schooling. Before long, the number of children rose to over 20 and eventually the couple applied for schooling status. The final number was almost 90 children. Many of the children were from broken homes and were emotionally in need of love and attention. For them the home school was a place of peace and security and the Lord ministered healing to them through this loving environment.

Life for Tony and Elsie has not always been easy, having to raise such a large family, but in Tony's words, "There has been much joy and God has always supplied our every need."

....

It was our privilege to have the young people coming to our home; each one was special and unique. More importantly, each one was very special to the Lord and He had a plan and purpose for their lives. Amongst the group were three members from the same family; they came from a difficult home situation and were constantly in our prayers. Each Saturday evening Mervyn would drive out in the car to pick up members for the weekly meetings. On many occasions he would knock on the door of the home where the three youngsters lived, only to be confronted with an angry parent informing him that the children were not coming. They were simply not allowed to attend that night and the door was closed.

One morning, after Mervyn had gone to work and the children had left for school, there was a knock at the front door. I left the sink where I was washing the breakfast dishes and went to the door. Standing there in tears, and in her school uniform, was a member of the abovementioned family. I took her in to the house and she shared a problem that had taken place in her home the night before. She had had little or no sleep and was due to sit an examination that morning. Feeling exhausted, she quite obviously felt ill prepared for the exam, and so, had called for prayer. I was thrilled to learn later that she had passed her exam with flying colours.

It was not unusual for the members of the group to call at our home during the course of the week, sometimes for prayer, sometimes just to share something. One young man had been pleading with me for a long while to make Koeksusters, (a South African cake recipe.) He came around one morning, mainly for fellowship, and stayed on to help me make them. In later years others came for piano and guitar lessons. Our home was always full of activity.

As the youngsters were always keen to spend time with one another, Mervyn and I decided to hold another week-end camp. But this time it would be under canvas in our front garden. Our minister and his family were on leave and we had been left in charge of the group. We felt that it would be a good opportunity for the young people to have quality time with each other.

We had just enjoyed a braaivleis, (a South African word for barbecue,) which was followed by the evenings programme. At 11 o'clock, after most of the members had gone to bed, four of us gathered together to end the evening with a short time of prayer. We prayed for a while and were then led to sing a song. Then we continued praying, and then sang another song. And so we continued on…and on…and on. We were not aware of the time passing, and we found ourselves sitting, then kneeling, then standing. We were totally caught up in the Lord's presence in our prayers and worship. After some time we were aware that another person had joined us, but it didn't disrupt our unity or time with the Lord; we just continued. I then became aware that there were tears among three of the group, then hugging, but the prayer and praise was not interrupted.

The Lord's presence was so very real, we were just caught up in our worship of Him. One of the group quietly suggested celebrating communion, and being very strongly led by the Holy Spirit we felt that this would be acceptable to Him. Without disrupting the flow of the Holy Spirit, some bread and water were quickly brought, and we celebrated together. The prayers and the worship continued on. Nobody was aware of the time, and it was just beautiful to be in the presence of the Lord in such a powerful way. Then, as suddenly as it had started, it stopped. As the Holy Spirit had come upon us, so He went.

We all opened our eyes together and looked at one another in amazement and wonder. A young man was sitting on the settee next to me, and he asked the time. I was astounded when I saw that it was four o' clock in the morning! We had been worshipping the Lord for five hours, and it seemed like half an hour. The young man sitting next to me said, "Oh, Mrs. Shaw, we didn't even clean up the kitchen after the braai." I replied, "Well, we didn't have a chance. We were only going to finish off the evening with a few minutes of prayer, and then clear up." We later learned that the person who joined us part way through was a young lady who had heard the singing, and as she wasn't able to sleep she decided to join us. The Lord had His reason for bringing her in, because there had been a broken relationship among the three members of the group, and in His perfect timing, He had brought them together in an atmosphere of love and acceptance to restore the relationship. At five o' clock we woke the rest of the group for their early morning quiet time. One young man stood in the door and said, "Wow! What's been going on in here? I can feel the presence of the Lord so powerfully!" It goes without saying that our further time of fellowship between five o' clock and six o' clock was one of great blessing. Again, everyone felt the power and presence of the Lord and their lives were touched in a very special and dynamic way. Thereafter that particular night was referred to as "The All-Night Prayer Meeting."

Several of the young people remarked how wonderful it would be if we could have another time the same. I explained to them that it was not something that could be engineered, but that it had been a very special work of the Holy Spirit. He chose to move in a new and beautiful way on that occasion, for His own reasons.

CHAPTER SIX

Blessings through Fellowship

"Behold, how good and how pleasant it is for brothers to dwell together in unity!" Psalm 133: 1

Mervyn and I had been involved with the leadership of the youth group for approximately two years, when, to our sheer joy, we learnt that it was now safe to return to Resthaven. Our prayers had been answered and the time had now come when it would be possible to hold a retreat in this beautiful valley.

Our journey out to Resthaven, this time, was to be the first of several retreats and conferences that we attended at the centre within the next few years. Spirits were running high and the young people could hardly contain themselves for sheer excitement as we approached the sign heralding the decent into the valley. "Resthaven, Come Ye Apart And Rest Awhile."

Several of the cottages, plus a dormitory, were booked for the group. We were approximately 30 in all, including adults and young people. All sessions and meals were held in the conference centre, which comprised a large hall with a kitchen added at one end. The hall was situated in a large open area surrounded by the beautiful indigenous Msasa and Mimosa trees. At intervals, dotted amongst the trees, stood the peaceful rustic cottages, and a little farther up the hillside, standing serenely by itself, stood the white chapel.

As I walked around, surveying the peaceful scene, taking in the sights and breathing in the familiar scents of the surrounding bush land, I distinctly remember thinking to myself, "It's a miracle that this beautiful centre has stood unscathed for so long." For many years the whole area surrounding the valley had been subjected to gunfire and threats of invasion. It was nothing short of a miracle that the centre, fully equipped and completely furnished, had been left untouched. There was no doubt in my mind that the Lord still had great plans for Resthaven.

The days that followed, although very busy, were days of fun and fellowship as we met together to worship the Lord and learn more about Him. The young people were keen to learn and participated fully in the activities, including kitchen duties. Even work is fun when spending time with friends and like-minded people.

Our times spent at Resthaven were always times of great blessing, both youth camps and church conferences alike. The following accounts have been taken from various times spent at the centre, and it is with grateful and thankful hearts that we praise God for His faithful and tangible presence with us at all times.

On one occasion I was working in the kitchen on a youth camp. Two young men, Alan* and Gordon*, were helping me. On the stove there was a pan of boiling oil, and, thinking it was water that should be thrown away, Alan lifted it and poured it down the sink. Unfortunately it went all over Gordon's arm. You can understand the seriousness of the situation. Immediately the group were called into the kitchen to pray. Shirley was a nursing sister and she attended to the arm with professional skill. We then prayed as a group, and asked for the Lord's healing. The oil had covered a large area, and most of Gordon's forearm should have blistered and been scarred. However, there was no blistering, and within a few days there was little evidence of a burn apart from a slight discolouration of the skin; and within two or three weeks the arm was completely clear. I was attending a "Lay Witness Mission" at our church some years later, and Gordon was with me in one of the small group discussions. One man asked, "Do you think that miracles still happen today?" Whereupon Gordon rolled up his shirtsleeve and told his story! There were about 15 cottages at Resthaven, and many of us preferred the cottage named

"Peace," for various reasons. One of the main reasons was that it was the largest, and slept 13 people comfortably, which meant that we had the opportunity to enjoy further fellowship during the evenings and between sessions. The Lord often chooses to minister to His people in the most unusual ways. One evening, following the last session of the day at a conference, when we had returned to our cottage, several of us were spending time in the Lord's presence. Quite suddenly and unexpectedly, three of us, Sue, Roberta and I, were hit with a spell of laughter. We laughed and laughed until our sides were aching, and the tears flowed. The incredible thing was that we could not stop, and it went on for an hour or two. Eventually we felt that we had to retire for the night. As Roberta was staying in another cottage she had none of her night things with her; nor did she have any of her medication, which she had to take. However, we felt that it was too late for her to go disturbing the other people in the cottage, so we found a spare bed in Peace, prayed for her health, about which Sue and I were somewhat concerned, and, still laughing, went to bed. A bout of continuous laughter as we had experienced can be very exhausting, but we also discovered a deep spiritual truth through it. The Lord had used it to minister to us in a very special way. Apart from the exhaustion we all felt "cleansed" and at peace within ourselves. We had been truly loosened up, and somehow, there was a new awareness of God's presence. I can only say that the experience was not of ourselves, and that God used it to minister to us in a very powerful way.

At another conference, while in a time of worship, the Holy Spirit moved so powerfully that the whole room full of believers found themselves prostrated on the floor before the Lord. It was a very moving experience and one could only feel a deep humility before our holy God.

On occasions speakers were brought up from South Africa to minister to us and we were also blessed to come under the teaching of several local ministers. It was a great privilege to listen to the word of God being proclaimed and expounded so powerfully.

The one thing that really spoke to me was that the fact that the speakers preached with expectant hearts. Having proclaimed the message, it was now time to act and stand upon the promises in God's word.

Therefore times of teaching and worship were followed by a time of ministry and the Lord honoured the faith and trust of His people by revealing Himself in signs and wonders. People received prayer for various needs; some were healed, many spoke in tongues and yet others fell under His power, (2 Chron. 5: 14); (Or, were "Slain in the Spirit," as it is known.) Nobody left a meeting without feeling a sense of awe and wonder at our mighty God.

As the knowledge of God's word was so important in our lives, much emphasis was placed upon memorising scripture. I have very strong memories of one speaker pacing up and down in front of us and repeating 1 Corinthians 1: verse 30 to us over and over and over again. "But by His doing you are in Christ Jesus, who became to us wisdom from God, and righteousness, and sanctification, and redemption..." in his mind it was imperative for us to learn this important portion of scripture and assimilate it into our lives.

It was always very special to meet up again with friends and acquaintances we'd met on previous conferences. Many life-long friendships were cemented at these important gatherings, and it was a blessing to continue to uphold one another in prayer during difficult times throughout the following years.

CHAPTER SEVEN

Provision in Crisis

"Now to Him who is able to do exceeding abundantly beyond all that we ask or think, according to the power that works within us." Ephesians 3: 20.

Although we lived in difficult times it was wonderful to experience the moving of God's mighty hand in so many different areas of our lives. One such time was during the course of a seven year drought.

The land was parched and dry, animals were dying for lack of water, people in the rural areas were suffering terribly and everyone was flagging under the intense heat. Salisbury's main water supply was from a dam approximately 30 kilometres outside the city, known as Lake McIlwaine. (This name was later changed to Lake Chivero.) Over the years the water level in the dam dropped alarmingly and people feared the worst. Eventually it actually dropped to just 13 per cent full. Large areas, which had once held thousands of gallons of water, were now just open spaces of squelchy mud. To look upon these once life-giving waters was in itself a tragedy, but what the empty spaces now revealed was even more frightening. Masses of weapons of war had been dumped into the waters during the previous years. Obviously those responsible for this had never expected this armament to be exposed.

Concern was not only for the fact that the main water supply for the city was down to 13 percent, but also because the pumping system was sorely in need of repair and was often inoperable. Spare parts had not been available to repair the system and we had basically been drinking "sludge" for a very long time. It had been necessary to purify all drinking water by boiling it. Constant prayer for this area was always needed.

The situation was desperate and Christians were called to a time of prayer and fasting. We had to pray for rain, although we had not seen any for many months. Faith had to be exercised; we were not even in the time of the official rainy season. We also realised that one good rainy season alone would not be sufficient to fill the dam, and were told by experts that it would take at least *three good* rainy seasons to fill the dam to capacity.

So hundreds of people across the land joined in prayer and fasting. After two or three weeks the clouds started to build up. Anyone who has lived in Africa will know the frustration and disappointment that comes before a downpour of rain. The clouds build up and up until the sky is black, one expects the rain to fall at any moment, but not a drop is to be seen. Instead, the sky clears and reverts to its normal deep blue, with not a cloud in sight. This happens repeatedly for days, or weeks on end and the heat is intense.

The prayers continued more fervently. Eventually, to everyone's joy, the drought broke and the rain came down in torrents. The intense heat gave way to temperatures that were more bearable and we praised God for relief. However, we continued to fast and pray, and day after day the rain fell unceasingly. We were praying for the impossible; this being, that the Lord would fill the dam to capacity in one season! We could not afford to pray for less, because anything short of the dam's full capacity would not carry the country through to the following rainy season.

We were used to the rain falling for a few days at a time, sometimes a week, and often in torrents. But what we were experiencing now was unheard of. Week after week it continued to pour down, both day and night. The dam level started to rise and people began to get excited. The sludge now gave way to water, which once again covered the reminders of a country at war. On occasions it was exciting to drive out to the dam, and join with many other people to witness this amazing miracle that was taking place before our eyes. For so many years, having seen more and more of the massive dam wall being exposed as the water level dropped, it was truly wonderful to see the surging waters rising above old water marks.

We were now in our sixth week of torrential rain. Slowly but surely the water crept towards the top of the dam wall. By this time the event had become headline news and even unbelievers were acknowledging God's hand in this amazing phenomenon. We were praying that the dam would actually spill.

As this possibility became more and more apparent the news media drove out to the dam in the evening and positioned themselves at the edge of the wall. At home we listened with great expectation to the broadcaster as he covered the events. His voice became quite excited as he reported that "the water is now lapping at the edge of the wall" and we could hear the crowds in the background cheering as they witnessed this spectacle. His voice came over loud and clear as the water spilled for the first time in years. "And now the first drops of water have spilled over the dam wall. Only God could have made this possible."

What an amazing answer to prayer! Man had said that "it would be impossible for the dam to fill in just one rainy season," (A rainy season lasts from three to four months) but God had filled it from 13 per cent full, to overflowing, in just six weeks!

After the dam had spilled the rain started to ease off and within days it stopped altogether.

Beryl Shaw

CHAPTER EIGHT

To the Glory of God

"And my God shall supply all your needs according to His riches in glory in Christ Jesus". Philippians 4:19.

As I have written the story of the building of the Hatfield Presbyterian Church in Harare in a previous publication, I will only refer to it briefly here; but because it was such an important time in our lives, I feel I cannot omit saying something about those life-changing years.

The church was built during 1979 and 1980. The Hatfield congregation was not an affluent one, but the members *did* believe in an affluent God. Important elements were in place for the work to proceed, and to be completed. Amongst the leadership there was a desire to build a church to the glory of God; they also believed that He had called them to carry out this work. Above all else great faith was present in the hearts of the leadership, a strong faith that believed in an all powerful, loving God who honours His word.

When building started there was about $6,000 available in the church account, and we had been given a quote of approximately $25,000 to complete the building. As this venture was an act of faith we prayed that the building would go up debt-free, and then started the work. A prayer group committed the needs to the Lord on a regular basis, and He supplied faithfully. We learned that we had to move forward at all times, believing that He would provide, and He never failed us. When we moved, God provided. When we stopped, the financial and material flow stopped. The building was completed in about a year and a half, and the final cost to the congregation was in the region of $40,000. Our prayers were answered, and we were free of any debt. God had provided all the way, and He was given all the praise and glory.

It was important to keep our eyes firmly fixed on the source of our supply, and above all else strict adherence to God's word. At one stage, an amount of $12,000 was needed. Consideration was given to obtaining a Building Society loan, but, unfortunately, a requirement was that somebody had to stand surety. Our minister stated that to accept a loan under such conditions would be contrary to God's word. (Prov. 11:15.) At the exact time that the church member returned to the Building Society to decline the loan, our minister had a visit from a person who made an offer of a loan of $12,000, interest free, and payable as and when convenient. This offer was accepted, and the person concerned later changed the loan to a donation, so nothing ever had to be repaid.

It was in this, and many other unexpected ways, that the Lord supplied for the building of the church. Each occasion was different and we learnt that God delights in surprising us. The miracle really was that if this project had been left to any one of us it would have been an impossible task, but God is a God of the impossible. He was the only One who knew how to move upon the heart of man to prompt him to give, or to make a phone call. He was the One who blessed His people with special gifts and raised them up for specific tasks, and He was the only One who knew where to find the right coloured bricks when they were in short supply, and at an affordable price!

As I look back and remember those times spent on the building, one thing that *never* ceases to amaze me is how the Lord protected all of us, especially the children. Month after month we worked untiringly, standing up on high ladders and scrubbing the outside brickwork with wire brushes, (three times around a large octagonal building!) laying bricks for pathways, painting walls and climbing scaffolding. All of this work was done with no fixed safety measures. The work seemed endless. The children, some as young as 2 years old, played around and about the rocky grounds by themselves, often running in and out of the church while the building was in progress.

It was quite obvious that the Lord had placed His angels within the building to watch over us; and in all the operations there were no serious accidents, although there were very many potentially serious ones. One young man fell from a very great height, hit the floor with a thud, picked himself up and walked out of the church without a word. He did not even suffer a bruise.

Throughout the months we also experienced healings. Shirley used to "man" the circular saw most ably. Month after month she cut the lengths of pine wood at various angles for the ceiling. One day, towards the completion of the building she came to me in the kitchen, held her finger in front of me and told me to pray for it! The saw had cut off a large piece of her nail, and she told me that she would not be able to play the organ for the service the next morning. I offered to bring the first-aid box, but she insisted that I pray first, which I did. The following morning I was shown the fingernail; it had grown back to its original length, and was completely healed.

It is amazing how often health problems can prevent people from undertaking some area of work. In my case, prior to the building of the church, varicose veins used to trouble me and standing for any length of time was something I was not able to cope with. However, I don't ever remember my legs aching, and never gave them a thought.

Only the Lord could have given me the courage when it came to climbing up scaffolding 20 feet high and then walking along a single plank to work on the pine ceiling. Initially I was petrified working at such a height. When sharing this story at a later stage, I discovered that I was not the only lady who had been afraid of heights; but somehow the Lord had given courage to each one of us, and this enabled the ladies to work alongside the men in completing this task.

Throughout the duration of the building there were numerous answers to prayer; supply, healing, provision of one kind or another. And with the completion of the church the members knew beyond any doubt that they served a living God, and that with Him, all things were possible.

CHAPTER NINE

Childlike Faith

But He said, "The things impossible with men are possible with God." Luke 18:27.

It was good to know that our children knew where to turn in times of need. On one occasion, during Karen's high-school years, she was confronted with a difficult situation. She needed to be in three places at once, and failing to be at any one of these would get her into trouble with someone. She committed the problem to the Lord, and asked for His help. Within a short while she was notified that the time of one of the appointments had been moved on. For personal reasons she made the decision to attend a particular one of the two remaining appointments, which was on the tennis courts, some distance from the school. It was customary for the teacher to call the roll starting from the beginning of the alphabet. As Karen stood in the queue she just asked the Lord to change the teacher's mind and start the roll-call from the end. Having the name of Shaw, it would mean that she would be free to leave much sooner. The teacher addressed the girls and said, "Just for a change, let's call the names from the end of the alphabet!" Karen was released from the tennis court, and arrived at the second appointment on time.

Most parents with sons are used to accidents of one form or another, and with three sons we have had our fair share. One morning, Kevin and Greg left for school on their bicycles. In an effort to warn some pedestrians Kevin rang his bell, but they did not respond. He swerved to avoid them, and hit a bump in the cycle track. He flew over the handlebars, and face first, landed on a rock. A few people gathered, and Greg, seeing his brother motionless, stood beside him and prayed. Not wanting to get into trouble at school for being late he then continued on, leaving Kevin in the care of others. Greg was about 8 years of age and Kevin 12.

Kevin was taken to hospital, where he regained consciousness. His face and the inside of his mouth were badly cut. As he was wheeled into surgery on a stretcher, he witnessed to the nursing staff how he had read in his Bible that morning that God would surround him and protect him. *"Fear not, for I am with you; be not dismayed, for I am your God. I will strengthen you, I will help you, I will uphold you with my victorious right hand."* (Isaiah 41:10 R.S.V.) *"Though I walk in the midst of trouble thou dost preserve my life; thou dost stretch out they hand against the wrath of my enemies, and thy right hand delivers me."* (Psalm 138:7 R.S.V.)

The cuts around Kevin's eyes were stitched up, but the doctor was reluctant to stitch the inside of his mouth and recommended that we take him to our dentist. After examination, the dentist, and other members of the staff felt that Kevin had had enough for one day, and suggested that we take him back for stitches the following morning. Kevin did not fancy the idea of returning to the dentist the following morning, and, unbeknown to me, asked his brothers and sister to pray for healing for him, which they promptly did.

The next morning my husband returned to the dentist with Kevin, and it was with sheer amazement that the dentist announced that Kevin's mouth had completely healed; the cut below his bottom teeth had been about four centimetres long. Many of the dental staff were called in to see the healing. To the astonishment of all, Kevin had neither pain nor bruising and refused to take any painkillers. He remained cheerful throughout.

During Craig's life he experienced numerous answers to prayer, especially throughout his school years. However, the one that I have chosen has been taken from his early working life. Once having started work all four of our children have saved and bought their own cars or motor bikes. Craig had now come to the point where he was looking to purchase a car, his specific prayer was for "one that would delight him!"

He saw a car that caught his attention parked on the forecourt of a garage – a two-tone Ford Capri. The price was beyond his reach, however, but this did not deter him and he started to fast and pray about it. Week after week he continued on, eating very little food at the end of each day. His face became thinner and thinner, and he became quite pale.

One or two other cars came up, but they were not to his liking. A story we were once told about persevering prayer is as follows: If we ask the Lord for roast beef and vegetables, and He initially offers us soup, we don't give up and settle for second best, accepting the soup. We persevere in faith and prayer until we receive that which we have prayed for. On one occasion, another car was available, and I asked Craig if he would consider it. He answered, "No Mum! It's the soup." And so he continued on, fasting and praying. Eventually the price of the Capri dropped a little, and then after a period of about three months the car disappeared. We presumed it had been sold, but within a short while my husband saw it parked at another garage. The price had been reduced even further, and now, having dropped by $6,000, was within Craig's reach. He was able to purchase it within a few days, and was "delighted" with it.

It was always a great comfort to know that we could take our various needs to the Lord, whether small or large. Nothing was beyond His help and we had learnt over the years that He was deeply concerned about every aspect of our lives.

One particular incident I recall was when Greg was writing important examinations for a graphic design course. He needed calligraphy pens and the only ones available were at an exorbitant price and were way beyond our reach, so once again the matter was committed to the Lord. As the time moved on Greg became quite anxious, saying that there was no way he could use the pens he had because they leaked, and there were only a few days to go before the exams, which were due to start on the following Monday. We continued to pray. On the Friday before the exams I received a phone call from a friend in Botswana (a neighbouring country). He phoned to ask if there was anything we needed as he had a rep coming through from Harare and returning on Sunday. The pens were requested, bought on the Saturday, and delivered to us on Sunday. Greg wrote his exams on Monday, did well, and passed.

There were many times that we prayed for specific medical concerns within the family and often had to wait for a number of years before we saw evidence of healing. One such time was when a number of young people were camping in our garden over a week-end. Late one afternoon Craig, then approximately 6 years old, was being given a ride on the back of a bicycle and he caught his foot in between the spokes of the back wheel. He was duly carried into the house and we examined his foot. The back of his heel had caught the brunt of the blow and, judging by the amount of skin that had been scraped off, it was evident that the heel had been quite damaged. Craig was a tough little boy and as he did not cry or complain about the pain; we were uncertain as to the extent of the injury. We considered taking him to the out-patients department of the hospital to have the injury checked, but as this was some distance away and his foot did not appear to be broken, we eventually decided to trust the Lord for the healing. We strapped the foot up, gathered everyone in for prayer and committed the injury to the Lord.

Approximately six years later, while on holiday, Craig jumped off of a low wall and twisted his ankle very severely. He could not walk on the foot at all. He was duly taken to a doctor and the ankle and foot were X-rayed. On this occasion Craig had severely torn the ligaments in his ankle and underwent many weeks of intense physiotherapy. However, the X-ray also revealed, that some years before, the heel had actually been cracked, but had healed perfectly.

As a family we paid regular six monthly visits to the dentist to have our teeth checked. When Greg was quite young we were once told that he had a calcium deficiency and in later years could expect problems with his teeth. We seriously committed this problem to the Lord and left it in His hands. A few years later, when Greg was being fitted for braces, the orthodontist found no evidence whatsoever of a calcium deficiency, and was even surprised when I mentioned it. Following a few years of wearing braces, his teeth were beautifully straightened with no difficulty at all, and have remained in perfect condition.

CHAPTER TEN

In His Strength Alone

"These things I have spoken to you, that in Me you may have peace. In the world you have tribulation, but take courage; I have overcome the world." John 16:33

The night before independence was to be announced in August 1980, I remember lying in bed talking to the Lord about the situation the country was facing. I was particularly praying for Mervyn, who at that time was away on call-up in the bush. We knew that Mr. Mugabe was coming to power, but none of us had any idea whatsoever what form independence was going to take. As I prayed for Mervyn's safety, plus the safety of hundreds of other men serving in the armed forces at that time, I was well aware that the following morning their lives could be taken by the new regime. In fact, not only theirs, but hundreds of other people, including myself, who had supported the ruling party at that time. I simply had to face the situation and trust the Lord with all of our lives.

What *did* actually take place the following morning was nothing short of a miracle. Mr. Mugabe simply commanded everyone to lay down their arms because, he said, "The country was now at peace!" Independence had been won. We, the wives at home, were quite overwhelmed as our husbands returned home to be with their families, this time for good.

Initially all appeared to be quiet in the country. Sadly we were unaware of the tragic circumstances that were taking place in another area just over 400 kilometres from us. We were not to learn until a few years later of the thousands of people of another tribe that had been annihilated.

Even though the country was "officially" at peace, this did not mean that we returned to an easy-going lifestyle. On the contrary, many changes were taking place and the need to keep our eyes fixed firmly on the Lord was of paramount importance. Thousands of people continued to leave the country every month, which threatened the security of every remaining family. However, at no time in all of these years did we consider leaving. The Lord had undertaken for us thus far and would continue to do so until He directed otherwise.

Adjusting to the changes taking place around us was not at all easy. The name of the country changed from Zimbabwe Rhodesia to Zimbabwe, and the city of Salisbury became Harare. Thereafter followed name changes of the towns and most of the main roads. These were named after political heroes and spirit mediums. It was not easy learning all of the new names; it was even harder to submit to using names of spirit mediums! But it was something we had to accept. Even the name of the general hospital was changed from the Andrew Fleming, (named after Dr. Andrew Fleming, Director of Medical Services in Rhodesia from 1896 - 1932) to the Parirenyatwa, (the name of a spirit medium). The name of the Lady Chancellor Maternity Home was changed to Mbuya Nehanda Maternity Home, (the name of another spirit medium).

Besides the name changes, important historical monuments were torn down. I think the one that affected us most, emotionally, was the statue of Cecil John Rhodes, which had stood in a prominent position in the city since its early formation. It was devastating to see the pile of rubble where once stood the proud statue of the founder of the country.

Everyone enjoyed the beauty and peace of Cecil Square, an attractive park which was located in the city centre. Many were the days I spent with the children sitting on the benches overlooking the colourful flower beds as we enjoyed a packed lunch. Adults and children alike shared the joy of watching the dancing fountains as they followed the changing patterns of the spray. Sometimes the spray went as high as five metres, or as low as 19 centimetres. At night time the fountains were lit up with coloured lights, which enhanced their beauty. The name of this garden changed from Cecil Square to Africa Unity Square, and sadly, within a few years, the once well- tended park became a thing of the past. Benches were broken, the fountains fell into disrepair and the lawns were strewn with rubbish. History was simply being eradicated before our eyes, and it was happening almost overnight.

Another thing that took some getting used to was learning to adjust to the new laws. One being, that while driving, in the event of hearing sirens warning of Mr. Mugabe approaching with his cavalcade, one had to *immediately* pull off to the side of the road and stop until the cavalcade had passed. On several occasions drivers were not quick enough to stop and were fired upon. I remember one poor lady was shot several times in her arm. It was only after several incidents like this that we really took in the seriousness of what was happening around us. The cavalcade consisted of outriders on motorbikes, several staff cars then Mr. Mugabe's car followed by further staff cars, an ambulance, armed vehicles and finally approximately a further eight motorbikes.

I remember, on one occasion when I was driving through the city I distinctly heard the sound of a siren. I was approaching a junction with traffic lights, but even though the green light was in my favour, thinking that the siren was warning of the president's approach, I immediately put my foot on the brake and came to an abrupt halt. Unfortunately the driver in the car immediately behind me was caught unprepared and ran into the back of the car I was driving (sadly our daughter's). As it happened the siren did not turn out to be that of the president, but of an ambulance. The driver behind me was most irate, especially as his car appeared to have sustained greater damage than mine. (Unfortunately further damage to Karen's car was discovered only after the case was closed.)

Police were called to the scene and promptly took statements, thereafter the drivers of both vehicles had to visit the police station to give written statements. This we duly did. My statement was accepted without further question as it was thought that I had made an acceptable mistake under the conditions of the law. Unfortunately the other driver was held responsible for the accident because he had run into the back of my car. He did try to fight the case for some length of time, but failed in his efforts. Eventually the case was closed.

Another incident that I recall involved of a friend of Mervyn's. Fred* was a registered firearms collector and all his weapons had been decommissioned by the police armoury. The firing pins had been removed, the mechanisms immobilised and the barrels blocked. However, in spite of his innocence of any crime, Fred was taken into custody for "possession of weapons of war." He was later released but his entire collection was confiscated.

Meanwhile, whilst all of these changes were taking place in the country, our daily routine continued on. As our children grew up and ventured into the working world, the Lord continued to lead and guide us with regards to their training and equipping, in areas most suited to their abilities and giftedness. It was amazing how He opened doors and provided opportunities for them to further their training and experience.

From a young age our three sons were involved in the Boys' Brigade and our daughter, Karen, in the Girls' Brigade. These organisations were affiliated to the Hatfield Presbyterian Church where we, as a family, were members. Although neither Mervyn nor I were leaders, the brigades played a huge part in our lives as a family, and Mervyn often drove the band to different venues. We fully supported our children and attended all their functions each year. All four children held active rolls within the organisations, and these, coupled with their involvement in the youth group (plus other extra-mural activities) kept them extremely busy.

After seven years we were led to bring the youth group to an end. Many of the young people had left for other countries, in most cases to further their training in specific fields. However, life continued on at a busy pace and our home continued to be full of activity. Apart from the busy lifestyle of the family members, other people were always coming and going, some for music lessons, others for Bible studies or prayer. For many years people of all ages had called for prayer. The Lord had revealed Himself as a mighty God and people came to trust in His unfailing love.

CHAPTER ELEVEN

Obedience in Prayer

At that time Jesus answered and said, "I praise Thee, O Father, Lord of heaven and earth, that Thou didst hide these things from the wise and intelligent and didst reveal them to babes." Matthew 11: 25

I would now like to relate an experience that I had with three other ladies in 1983. We were led to pray for eight senior Air Force officers who had been accused of sabotage following a fire at one of the Air Force bases, (we believed they were innocent,) and who were now on trial. If they had been found guilty the penalties would have been very severe. The trial ran for nine months, during which time we met at the church almost every morning of the week.

During our time of prayer we all felt a very strong concern for two of the men, one more so than the other. We passed the names of the men to a friend who was connected with the case. He was concerned specifically with the spiritual welfare of the men. After a few days he came back to us, and asked if we thought it would be possible to go back to the Lord and ask Him to confirm our thoughts concerning one man. I remember saying, "Well, Gideon did." I suggested we fast on that day, and the ladies agreed. At the start of our time of prayer I suggested we cover the day's proceedings at the court, and then go into an hour of silent prayer during which time we would write down any thoughts that came to us. Also, I mentioned that we should feel free to move around the church. We had actually been given the names of three men to pray for, but only one was to be confirmed by the Lord.

We went into a time of silent prayer, and after a short while two of the ladies moved to the front of the church. (We used to sit in the sun at the back of the church in the winter months!) A few minutes passed and then the one lady with me suggested we move to the front of the church and join the other two, which we did. All four of us knelt at the base of the steps in front of the communion table. I personally was expecting the Lord to write the name of the man on the wall in front of us, and so I knelt with my eyes open watching for a long while for the writing to appear! As nothing happened I thought I had better close my eyes. I centred my thoughts upon the Lord, and after a short while I clearly "heard" (in my mind) His voice say to me, "Dare you come before My throne of grace?" I replied, "Yes Lord, I am a child of the Living God." Again, I heard the voice, "Dare you come before My throne of grace?" Again I replied, "Yes Lord; I am a child of the Living God, and I have been saved by grace." Still a third time it came, "Dare you come before My throne of grace?" and so I replied for the third time, "*Yes* Lord, I am a child of the Living God and I have been saved by grace, and cleansed from my sins by the blood of Your Son Jesus Christ." I continued to centre my thoughts upon the Lord, and then I heard the voice again, "Take off your shoes; you are standing on holy ground."

I was busy thinking about this when the words were repeated. I was a little unsure whether I should actually take my shoes off when the voice came for the third time, and this time in a commanding tone. I felt that I should be obedient, and so removed my shoes. I continued to kneel and stay quiet before the Lord, and then the voice came again, "Prostrate yourself before Me." I was very hesitant! When the words were repeated I said, "You know, Lord, I've never done this before in front of the ladies," and the reply came, "Well, you'd better get used to it. You will be doing it again soon in front of a far larger crowd. Prostrate yourself before Me!" I had no alternative but to be obedient. As I opened my eyes to lie myself down, I noticed that the lady next to me had taken her shoes off, and also those of her little girl, and was kneeling. I remained prostrate on the floor for a while, and eventually the voice came again, "You can get up now." I rose to a kneeling position. I continued to centre my thoughts on the Lord, but after a while, due to tiredness, my head dropped down, and the voice returned, "Look up." Each time my head dropped I heard the voice, "Look up. Look at my cross!" I opened my eyes and fixed my gaze on the cross in front of me on the communion table, and also on the cross-shaped window at the front of the church. Eventually I thought I had better start praying for the three men. I named the first before the Lord, but before I had time to continue the voice came, "You needn't worry about him; he is in the palm of My hand." I moved on to the next name, and heard the same words again. I then named the third man, and I clearly heard, "Write it down." I asked, "What if I am wrong Lord?" but again, "Write it down." So I wrote it down and concentrated on this man in prayer. I then felt led to write more, which I did.

After a few more minutes I heard movement, so opened my eyes to see that the ladies were moving to the back of the church. As I was not wearing a watch I presumed that the hour must be up, so put my shoes on, and went to join the others. As I neared them one said, "He kept telling me to be obedient," and the lady replied, "I am, Lord, I am." Another said, "Well, He kept telling me to look up," and the third said, "Well, He told me to take off my shoes because I was standing on holy ground." And yet another remarked, "Well, He told me to prostrate myself before Him." And so we discovered that we had all received the same instructions, and, praise the Lord, had all been obedient. We had all written down the same name, and the words of prophecy were all similar, and confirmed one another. One lady had been told to lie on her back. She was a little unsure but did so. I have often praised the Lord that she heard His voice correctly and was obedient, because the next day she was ordered by her doctor to lie on her back for three weeks as she was threatening a detached retina! A prophecy received later that day confirmed that the instructions given to the group had been a test of obedience.

The confirmed name of the man was passed to our friend, who was later able to share with us that it was correct, and that the concern had been that he would break down on the witness stand. We were then able to increase our prayer coverage for him, and the Lord upheld him.

At the end of the trial the eight men were found "Not guilty."

Referring to the Lord's instruction to me, "that I had better get used to prostrating myself before Him, because I would be doing it in front of a larger crowd;" I soon found how true this was. Within two or three months of this experience I found myself on a conference where a room of approximately 40 people were all prostrate before the Lord! (This incident has been mentioned in a previous chapter.)

CHAPTER TWELVE

Ministering in the Power of the Holy Spirit

"Praise Him with the sound of the trumpet; praise Him with the psaltery and harp. Praise Him with the timbrel and dance: praise Him with stringed instruments and organs."
Psalm 150: 3, 4. (K.J.V.)

Just before the closure of the youth group we had already started taking the young people to sing at a nursing home in Harare. The mother of one of the members of the group lived there, and this was our initial contact. At the end of the same year, 1985, a larger group of people went from the church to sing Christmas carols at the nursing home and hospitals. I felt very strongly that the Lord was calling the group to a deeper commitment to this work, and I shared this with the members. Everyone had a complete witness to the idea, and so it was committed to the Lord in prayer. A decision was made to form a group, and, following a further time of prayer, a name for the group was given, "Living Light." This was then followed by a confirmation from John 8: 12, *"Again therefore Jesus spoke to them, saying, "I am the light of the world; he who follows Me shall not walk in the darkness but shall have the light of life."*

With the formation of the song group, the years that followed were times of great joy and blessing. Practices were held in our home and were generally preceded by a bring and share lunch. Programmes comprising readings, songs and testimonies were taken on a regular basis, and also at Christmas and Easter, to a number of homes and hospitals in Harare. Many of the younger members played a variety of instruments including trumpet and cornet, flute, clarinet, guitars, drums, keyboard and a bell lyre. Prior to the commencement of programmes and during intervals, where pianos were available, some of the members entertained the residents in the nursing homes by giving a recital.

During this time of ministry the Lord's presence was made very real to us. The Living Light song group became a very close-knit group of people as a result of the constant fellowship and prayer. Three whole families were included in the group, which consisted of just over 20 people. Their ages ranged from approximately 12 years old to over 40. Friends were also welcome to join us as we visited various venues, and they derived much enjoyment as they participated in the programmes. Our presence, at the nursing homes especially, was welcomed with warm appreciation as many of the residents had very few visitors, or often none at all. In many cases their families had left the country; this, and the added problem of travelling vast distances, plus shortages of fuel, had left them isolated. It was a joy to see the faces of the elderly and infirm as they watched the young people in the group, and participated in the songs and hymns that they knew.

Following a programme, we were often surprised at the comments from some of the residents. Within the group we were always aware of the Lord's presence as He undertook for us, especially during the sharing of testimonies. I remember one lady in particular telling me how she "very much enjoyed listening to a particular instrument." No matter how much I tried to tell her that we didn't actually have that particular instrument in the group, she nevertheless *insisted* that she'd heard it! Through this, and other similar comments, I came to realise just how very much the Lord loved these people, and to what extent He would go to meet the desires of their hearts. If the resident loved that particular instrument so much, then He was quite prepared to provide the sound for her enjoyment, and I had no doubt that she had heard the instrument.

Often, in our times of prayer before entering a venue, the Lord would reveal Himself through a vision, or a word of knowledge or encouragement. He knew our weaknesses and limitations, and we ourselves knew our need of complete dependence on Him. The group looked to me as their leader, but I, in turn, with my limited knowledge of music, leaned heavily upon the Lord. We praise God that He never failed us, but on the contrary, far exceeded our expectations of what He would do amongst us.

On one occasion we were practising a song called "The Foot-washing Song" for our Easter programme "Resurrection Joy." As I prayed about the song I felt that it would take on a deeper meaning to the members if they participated in a foot-washing ceremony. Feeling very strongly led by the Lord in this, I shared the idea with them at one evening's practise. After a time of prayer I brought a bowl of water and a towel, and we proceeded to wash one another's feet. We were gathered in circle in our lounge, and each one washed the feet of the person on their right. The ceremony was a most moving experience; during the washing one felt a great love for his brother or sister in Christ. The group was truly united during the time of praise and the practise that followed. The exercise enabled the members of the group to identify with the love of Jesus for His disciples. The desired effect was captured, and the song was entered into with love and enthusiasm.

A few days after this incident, I learnt an amazing thing. One member shared with me that he had been quite horrified at the thought of having to take his shoes and socks off in public as he was suffering from a skin complaint on his feet. Under these circumstances, understandably, the thought of someone washing his feet was very threatening. However, he obediently submitted to the suggestion, faced the challenge and the Lord undertook for him. To his sheer amazement he learnt very soon afterwards that the skin complaint had cleared! I was once again reminded of God's almighty love and compassion for His children, and how, when we are obedient and submissive to Him, we open the way for Him to pour out His blessings in the most unexpected ways.

There were many moving testimonies given in the programmes. People testified to God's provision in their lives, His strength in times of weakness, of healings, and of miraculous interventions in times of danger. The testimonies were always encouraging to listen to, and, above all, served to increase and strengthen the faith of those sharing.

I would like to share the following testimony, which was given by our daughter Karen at the time of entering full-time service with the Girls Brigade in February 1987.

KAREN'S TESTIMONY

"I'm going to be sharing on abundant Life, on blessings that come beyond abundance when we live a life dedicated to Him.

I think as most of you probably know I work for the Girl's Brigade. I started there in February last year (1987), and it was not what I expected. I thought that because a person was working for God it would be easy to just go in to the office and get on with the work, and everything would fall into place. Somehow it would be great, and yet I didn't seem to fit into that category when I started.

It was quite a shock because I came into a situation where there was already one girl working in the office, and I was just told, "Work with her." She didn't give me any work; nobody gave me any work. Because there wasn't a place for me to be I was put into a back room. It was all cluttered and was an absolute mess, filthy dirty and with only one tiny little window, so I had to have the light on all day. It was rather a terrible shock to start off like that.

In the room there was a beautiful wooden badge mounted on a stand; we still have it in our office now. It's a lovely piece of work and it was the one nice thing in the office. One day, after I'd been there for just over a week, I was having my early morning quiet time. I'd read a passage in the Bible and I was praying about it. I was praying about work and saying, "Lord, I'm in the office but I've got nothing to do. What must I do with my whole day and how can I get on with the other girl?" Then He brought to my mind the words that I had just read in 2 Corinthians 4: 16 – 18, "Therefore we do not lose heart, though outwardly we are wasting away, yet inwardly we are being renewed day by day. For our light and momentary troubles are achieving for us an eternal glory that far outweighs them all. So we fix our eyes not on what is seen, but on what in unseen. For what is seen is temporary, but what is unseen is eternal." (N.I.V.) and I thought "Well that's great, life can only be trouble! But I don't feel very renewed Lord." I read it again, "But we fix our eyes not on what is seen." And as I read "what is seen," my office came to mind, all junky, gloomy and dirty. I saw the other girl there, and I saw this wooden badge on its stand, which actually looked pretty dull amidst all the mess. I read on further, "But we fix our eyes on what is unseen." As I read "unseen," I saw myself in heaven with Jesus standing in front of me, and behind Him was a huge badge, the Girl's Brigade badge. It was *huge;* it was so wide and it was at least three times as high as me. It was all shimmering, red and blue and gold, and it was bright and shining. As I looked up at it, I looked up at the cross and I saw Jesus standing there. The cross on the badge stands for Jesus; I saw Him standing in front of me all in white. I looked up to see the crown and it wasn't there because the crown was actually on Jesus' head. So I looked below to see the lamp, and that wasn't there either, because the lamp is the Word of God and Jesus is the Word of God, so there's no need for the lamp.

We too are like a lamp kneeling at the cross waiting to be filled, and I was already there, kneeling at Jesus' feet waiting to be filled. I looked behind to see if the torch was at the top, the flame, symbolising the Holy Spirit and there was no need for that either because the Holy Spirit's presence was all around us who were there. I looked to see then if the red background, the blood, standing for salvation, was there, and it was not there either because we who were there had already been saved.

Lastly, my attention was drawn to the two gold circles surrounding the badge. The inner circle representing the fellowship of Girl's Brigade around the world and the outer circle representing the fellowship of the church. Once again, neither of these was visible. There was no longer any need for them because we were all united in Christ. All that was left was the cross, with just me kneeling at Jesus' feet with Him wearing His crown and being in His rightful place as King.

And that's all that really matters in our lives; we should be kneeling at Jesus' feet with Him as our King. And truly I can say that the badge became very real, because the badge will go on forever, not as a symbol, but in its reality, because it's eternal and really we can only be truly filled and truly blessed when we give all to God. When I go along in a half-hearted way I don't really enjoy life that much. But when I put everything in it for God, and I go all out for Him, I get so excited and I really enjoy life that way, and I find such blessing after giving all to God and going wholly for Him."

···

We were very grateful to those who were willing to share their testimonies. Listening to the wide range of experiences brought by all ages, always served to remind us that God was ever present in our personal lives.

CHAPTER THIRTEEN

Fearlessly Trusting

He who dwells in the shelter of the Most High will abide in the shadow of the Almighty. I will say to the Lord, "My refuge and my fortress, My God, in whom I trust!" Psalm 91: 1, 2.

During the course of these years our family was deeply grateful to have the warmth and support of God's people, particularly those in the Living Light song group, with whom we had become very close. Constant change was taking place all around us and unexpected things happened overnight in our lives. One such thing was the sudden arrest of many innocent people, including my husband. Although this was devastating to us as a family it was evident that the Lord was with us every step of the way. It is important to draw attention to this event because it was all part and parcel of our everyday lives. People were suffering all around us for various reasons, but life continued on and the Lord gave us strength from one day to the next. The children coped in school and at work, and the Living Light song group continued to minister to the sick and elderly

We knew beyond a shadow of a doubt that God was in control and that He would work all things out for the good of our family. His plans were for good and not for evil. Many years later we can testify to the truth of this promise and give all praise to God for His mighty power.

The following testimonies were written during this period and illustrate how God undertook for us in these circumstances.

Testimony of God's Power and Provision

Beryl Shaw

"God is our refuge and strength, a very present help in trouble." (Psalms 46:1).

These were the first words that came to me when my husband was arrested at 2 a.m., on the 7th July 1986. I was very glad to know that God was with me and my family as my husband was driven away. I knew that, as always, the Lord was in control, and that He had a reason for allowing this to happen. I praised Him for His word which says, *"Beloved, if our heart does not condemn us, we have confidence before God"* (1 John 3:21); and so I knew that although we had been told "fraud in the office" we would be able to stand on God's word and claim this promise for my husband, knowing that he was innocent, and know also, beyond any shadow of a doubt that God would fight for us as He tells us in Exodus 14:14.

Before he left home, my husband phoned a friend; we felt that we should at least tell someone. Within half an hour of my husband leaving, the friend arrived and we spent the next hour or so talking and drinking tea. I remember telling our friend about the last time the Lord had miraculously protected us, about three years before, and I know that because of the amazing way He had intervened at that time, He was quite capable of doing so again. We did not know where my husband had been taken to, but our friend said he would try to locate him later that day. Meanwhile, my husband had left the name of a lawyer with me and I was to contact him as soon as possible. At 6 a.m., I placed our situation on the Prayer Chain and within a short while many people were praying. The children took the news very well and I reassured them that as the Lord knew their father was innocent He would fight for us. We now look back over the past two years and realise just how much fighting He did do for us, and how many miracles He had performed.

At 7 a.m., another friend from the congregation called and assured us of his support and help in any way. Then our two sons ages 11 and 13 left for school, and our daughter and other son left for work. I also left home to keep a dentist's appointment at 8 a.m., as I felt it would serve no purpose to cancel the appointment and have to wait possibly for weeks for another one. Also, I knew that no one knew the whereabouts of my husband, or the four other men who had been arrested at the same time. In an attempt to be as quick as possible, I shared the situation with the dental assistant who attended to me immediately. She was shocked at the news and stated that "I must be in a state!" I replied that I wasn't as the Lord knew where my husband was and He was with him and was in control of the situation.

I left them within half an hour and returned home. I phoned the lawyer who had heard of what had happened, but he had no idea of the whereabouts of any of the men. During the morning I received many phone calls from people assuring me of their support and prayers. One call was from a lady I had heard of but never met. When I answered the phone she simply stated her name very briefly, and then gave the following references:

Psalm 35:11, 12 *"Malicious witnesses rise up; they ask me of things that I do not know. They repay me evil for good, to the bereavement of my soul."* And also from Psalm 35, verses 27 and 28: *"Let them shout for joy and rejoice, who favour my vindication; and let them say continually The Lord be magnified, who delights in the prosperity of His servant. And my tongue shall declare Thy righteousness and Thy praise all day long."* The support of the body of Christ was felt immediately and it was so good to know that people cared. Later that day our friend called to say that he had located my husband: actually he was just down the road in our local police station, and that I would be able to take him a meal that evening! The children and I were so pleased and really praised the Lord. Our friend accompanied me when I visited my husband in the evening and I was able to spend a short while with him. My husband was confused, shocked and very annoyed. The following day the lawyers started proceedings for bail. Many people were praying continually and during the day I received a beautiful card with a reference from Psalm 77:14 on it: *"Thou art the God that workest wonders."* We continued to stand on God's promises and at 4:30 p.m., the men were released on bail. One friend had turned up with a large sum of money in his pocket, willing to assist anyone who needed financial help. Two other people were standing by to pay my husband's bail. The Lord is good, indeed.

The five men were suspended from work, which meant quite simply "no work...no pay" and so we started to pray for employment while the men reported to the police stations daily. Within two days a friend asked my husband if he would consider assisting him in running a "Take-Away" business that he owned, as he urgently needed the help. My husband started working there and continued to work there for the following year. We later learned that our friend had been praying for a man to take over as manager so that he would be released to return to his former work. The year spent at the "Take-Away" was one of the happiest years of my husband's working life. He was working among Christians in a very pleasant atmosphere. Our friend was concerned over the salary he was able to offer, but when praying about it the Lord had assured him that "the Body will make up the amount needed," and this is exactly what did happen.

We ourselves had cut down on our monthly expenses, and as we live on a cash basis there were no accounts to worry about. The men continued reporting to their respective police stations daily, but later the conditions were changed to reporting weekly. After two months this came to an end and thereafter the men simply reported to the court, and were remanded from one month to the next. This continued until November 12th 1987, when the case finally came to trial. By this time a further three men had been suspended, making eight in all.

During these 16 months the Lord continued to undertake for our family in the most amazing ways. Whenever we had extra expenses to meet, we seriously considered selling something from our home, and were quite prepared to do so. But before it ever got to that stage, the Lord would supply a gift of money to cover the need. These gifts ranged from $10 to $5,000! To relate all of these incidents would take a full book, and there is not enough time for that at this stage, but I will share a few examples. On one occasion we were praying for $40 to meet a telephone account, which had to be paid by the following day. As we were going in to our church that morning my husband asked if I knew how we were going to get to a particular nursing home that afternoon as our fuel gauge was registering empty. (We take a group of people to sing to the elderly in the homes.) I replied that it was in the afternoon, and we would worry about it when the time came. When the service ended we were handed an envelope containing $50! This covered the phone bill and the fuel needed as well.

We actually received 30 to 40 envelopes in the same way during these months. On another occasion we were praying for $1,000 for car repairs;

this came in the form of a cheque, through the post....exactly $1 000. At one stage we were praying for $2,000 for lawyer's fees, plus a few hundred to meet school fees. We were given a gift of $5,000! This continued throughout the whole of the 16 months. There was just one occasion when the Lord led us to gather a few miscellaneous items from around our home, and take them to the auctions. We were praying for a figure of $607 for school fees. The amount realised from the auctions was $607.25. As one of our children said, "I wonder what the 25 cents was for." In all this time the Lord provided for us over and above our needs, and one of the most valuable lessons He taught us in all of this was how to live on a lower income, and still be able to give and share ourselves. Our family have been in the habit of tithing for a number of years, and we rejoice in the knowledge of His word which says, *"Give, and it will be given to you; good measure, pressed down, shaken together, running over, they will pour into your lap. For by your standard of measure it will be measured to you in return."* (Luke 6:38).

Another way in which the Lord has provided for our family is in the area of transport. Due to lack of spares our car has been in the garage for a year and a half, yet whenever we have needed transport urgently a friend has either left a car with us while on leave, or others have been willing to lend their vehicles for specific needs.

Many friends continued to pray throughout this time, not only in Zimbabwe, but also in S.A., the U.K., and Australia as well. We are so grateful to them all. One family in South Africa even made our family their special prayer project. Many prayer meetings in Harare upheld our family before the Lord, and one particular meeting will always remain in our memories as a very special and blessed time. We had reached a very critical point in the investigation of our case, and so a special prayer meeting was called by a member of our congregation. As this family could not accommodate all the people in their lounge, they decided to hold the meeting in one of their stables: Thirty people turned out on a freezing cold night, and a very precious time was spent with the Lord and one another, in praise, prayer, and intercession for our family. The stable was lit by hurricane lamps, and we all sat in a circle on bales of hay.

One very significant thing that I remember happening very soon after my husband was suspended, was simply that we were very sorry that we were unable to let family and friends overseas know of our situation; and so the Lord brought them to us, or took members of our family to them, often in the most amazing ways. One friend had an hour's stop-over in Harare while travelling from South Africa to the U.K., and just decided to spend the hour with us. On another occasion, our daughter won a scholarship with the Girls' Brigade and spent four months in the U.K.

After working for a year at the Take-Away, the business was sold and the Lord provided part-time work for my husband until the trial. Three days before the trial the Lord showed us that He was preparing my husband for a new life; the references He gave us were John 12:24: *"Truly, truly, I say to you, unless a grain of wheat falls into the earth and dies, it remains by itself alone; but if it dies it bears much fruit."* And 1 Corinthians 15: 36: *"You fool! That which you sow does not come to life unless it dies."* We had no idea what lay ahead, but knew that the Lord had a new life ahead for my husband. The three days that followed were some of the hardest for him.

On advice given by their advocate the men pleaded guilty, going completely against everything they believed and knew to be true. They were told they would receive fines and suspended sentences. There was a faint chance of a short, three-month imprisonment, but this chance was almost totally discounted.

On the third day of the trial I accompanied my husband to the court. Before entering it he gave me his watch, hugged me and said "Cheers". Although things looked bleak for us I continued to believe in a miracle, knowing that the Lord could intervene even at the last possible moment. When sentence was passed my husband received four years with hard labour. Eighteen months of the sentence was suspended, and he would get a third off for good behaviour, leaving an effective 22 months to serve.

The Lord's hand was upon us in that courtroom and He miraculously undertook for us. For me, it was as if I had a cushion in front of me softening the blow. As I looked at my husband a shaft of light was shining down on his head and I was reminded of the words the Lord had given me months before, *"And He will bring forth your righteousness as the light, and your judgement as the noon day."* (Psalm 37 v 6). And I knew that in His good timing the Lord would honour His word for my husband.

Our two oldest children were with me, and the Lord upheld and strengthened us as we left the courtroom with our friends. I remember saying to our minister, "And He will still bring forth his righteousness as the light and his judgement as the noonday." The whole courtroom was shocked at the sentence and the lawyers just sat shaking their heads, unable to take in what they had just heard. I returned home to break the news to our two youngest children. It was not easy but the Lord undertook for me. They were both broken-hearted. Our minister and his wife called, and then I took the children to visit my mother-in-law and tell her the news. On the way home I remembered my husband's watch in my handbag and knew that I must give it to our youngest son who had saved for months for a watch, but had been unable to buy the type he wanted as it was unavailable in the country. In the evening I told him I knew his daddy would want him to have his watch, either until he was able to buy his own, or his dad came home.

One of the questions that the youngest one asked me was. "Will you have to go out to work now?" I have always been at home with our children, so I replied that we would not make any decisions immediately, but would pray about it. At approximately 7 p.m., that evening about a dozen people from the congregation arrived at our home and filled our kitchen with groceries. We were also given an envelope containing over $1,200. Even the children in our congregation had contributed to the gift.

When I went to bed that night I found an envelope under my pillow. It contained letters to me and the children from my husband. It was obvious that the Lord had prepared him, and before he left home he knew that he would not be returning that day. In my letter he wrote, "I have left my watch behind as I will not be able to wear it; please give it to Craig. He can have it until he can buy his own, or I come home! On reading his letter, our oldest son remarked, "It is as though dad knew he was going." I replied, "He did."

Next morning I received a call to say that a fund had been started and that it would support our family for as long as was necessary. I then had the answer to my son's question; no, I would not have to go out to work, but could continue on looking after my children and being involved in the Lord's work from my home. The hand of the Lord was on the fund, and it was contributed to by many people from Zimbabwe, South Africa, Malawi and England. Many who did not even know us contributed.

Apart from the fund we had many offers of help; one elderly lady offered help with the school fees, another family offered to buy the boys' clothes. (I did not take up either of these offers as the Lord supplied through the fund, and other gifts of money.) One family paid $150 for a term's bus tickets, some one else paid one of our children's tennis fees, and another their library subscriptions. (I used to receive an account complete with receipt.) We received one gift specifically for their music lessons. Another family started growing extra vegetables, and someone else provided a bag of vegetables weekly. Milk tokens, eggs and groceries poured in continually, as did numerous beautiful cards and letters from many places. The children and I joined in prayer for my husband every night and the Lord gave us strength. We knew that He was in control and would bring good out of this whole situation as He promises in His word. How I praised Him. We knew that His word says, *"For my thoughts are not your thoughts, neither are your ways my ways declares the Lord. For as the heavens are higher than the earth, so are my ways higher than your ways, and my thoughts than your thoughts."* (Isaiah 55: 8, 9)

We knew that it didn't matter how bleak the situation looked to human eye, because God viewed things very differently, and worked things out in ways we couldn't even dream of.

Two days after my husband was taken to prison, I was able to visit him in the morning for 15 minutes. I was accompanied by our minister and a friend. I felt desperately sorry for my husband; his hair had been completely shaved off, according to regulations, and he was broken-hearted. He was sleeping with 74 other men, on the floor, in a cell that had originally been designed to accommodate 25 persons; food was inadequate, and what was provided was inedible. We immediately started praying that the Lord would improve the conditions. This prayer was answered within four days, in the form of a move to another prison, a maximum security one, also in Harare. Living conditions were immensely better and my husband now had a bunk to sleep on, and blankets as well, although they were totally threadbare. There were fewer people in each cell; only 28 in a cell designed for 12. We continued to pray for the food. Visiting conditions were very hard - one person, once a month, for 15 minutes only, and we were separated by glass, speaking on a telephone.

On Saturday 14th November 1987, the same day that I visited my husband for the first time, a Boys' Brigade display and an open day was being held in our church in the afternoon. As our three sons were all involved and receiving various awards it was necessary for us to attend. The Lord stood by and gave to each one the strength they needed. Our eldest son led the band, and people said that they had never heard the band play so well before.

As I sat through the afternoon my thoughts were very much on the evening that lay ahead. Our family are involved in a ministry of song to the elderly, and that evening the programme was being presented to the church. The title of the programme, which had been running for a few weeks was "God is in Control". We knew full well that God was in control, yet were still very much aware that we would need His strength to carry us through the evening. As I left the church after the Boys' Brigade display I said to the Lord, "Well, Lord, I don't know how you're going to give me the strength, but I know you're going to do it."

From the time I left the church that afternoon, a peace and strength came upon me in a way that I had never experienced before. During a time of prayer before the programme our daughter broke down and was immediately prayed for by the group. A peace came over her, and she said, "It's all right now. I know that Dad's alright." A new strength took hold of her and during the programme she testified to God's control and provision in our situation. The power of God that came upon the group that night had to be experienced to be believed. My voice was stronger than I had ever heard it before and everybody present marvelled at the presence and power of God.

I remember our youngest son's reading so well: "If God's ways and thoughts are so much higher than ours then we should not be surprised at some of the things that happen in our lives; and we should not strive to understand exactly what is taking place, for He alone knows all the details. We are told to *"Walk by faith and not by sight"* and so we find strength in the promises of God. We read in Jeremiah 29:11, *"For I know the plans I have for you says the Lord. They are plans for good and not for evil, to give you a future and a hope."*

Meanwhile, the Lord continued to undertake with the visiting. A friend was also allowed to visit once a month in his capacity as a policeman. In addition to this, the Lord moved mountains and made it possible for three ministers to visit once each during the second month. This in itself was a miracle. I had originally been advised that I would be allowed to take two children in with me, and so for the first two months I did so. However, when a change of guard occurred this was stopped, and I discovered that the correct ruling was no children between the ages of 7 and 18. Our two youngest were not eligible to visit yet had visited their father three times. The Lord had simply made it possible.

I was also allowed to take the children over the Christmas period, and at this time we were also allowed to take in food.

My husband's diet consisted of two slices of bread at 7:30 a.m., which was breakfast, a small boiled potato (only edible on two occasions) at 11:30 a.m., which was lunchtime, and for supper which was at 2:30 p.m., another small potato and some meat. The meat consisted of a chicken's head, or foot, a pig's tail, or a piece of fat. When on rare occasions vegetables were provided, they were rotten, and too bad to eat. The children and I saw some of these vegetables being delivered to the prison, and realised that they were bad before even arriving. After supper the prisoners were locked back into the cells until the next meal, which was breakfast the next morning.

We were praying for my husband's health, and one of the ways the Lord answered was to supply apples for him in a most amazing way. The prisoners were issued with 10 cigarettes each per week, and as my husband is a non-smoker he used his cigarette ration to purchase apples from the other prisoners. Each prisoner was given one apple per week, and my husband was eating up to 10 a day.

There were times when we did experience difficulties with visiting, and our two eldest children were turned away on two or three occasions, for differing reasons. This was very hurtful, after waiting for a month or two to see their father. Our eldest son did not actually get in to see him and speak to him over the telephone until one week before his father's release. Visiting at Christmas and New Year was conducted through two fences about 6 meters apart. Guards were patrolling between the fences and they passed the food through to the prisoners after it had been tested and tasted either by themselves or us.

On New Year's Eve a praise and prayer evening was held at our home to commit the new year to the Lord. The evening ended just after midnight, and I got to bed at 1 a.m. I was up again at 4 a.m., to clean the house, and at 5:30 a.m., I was making hamburgers for my husband, something he had said he would like. Unfortunately, on arriving at the prison, we were told that no food was allowed, contrary to what I had been told, and that only one person was allowed to visit. Making the decision in a hurry, I went in to see my husband, and the children waited outside, very disappointed and upset. Sadly, I realised afterwards that I should have let our daughter visit her father, as this was just before her 21st birthday.

This was the most painful and hurtful experience of all, especially for my husband, our daughter's 21st birthday on the 5th of January. There was just no way that we could get her in to see her father, and of all that had happened this was the one that we had the greatest difficulty in understanding. It just did not seem possible that after 21 years of bringing her up, my husband could be away under such strange circumstances. It was the darkest time of all for him. We could only accept that the Lord had His own reasons.

The Lord had shown us that my husband had been set apart, and would die to himself and to his old life, and be raised to a new life. This was exactly what was happening to him. He had been unjustly convicted and was torn apart within himself over being taken from his family. And yet, through it all, he continued to praise and thank God for it all, knowing that it was for his own good.

Daily he spent hours studying the word of God, and wrote many meditations and prayers. Our friend visiting, continually marvelled at his attitude, and always came away from my husband feeling uplifted himself. He went to cheer and came away cheered. Prisoners are allowed to write only one short letter a month, and my husband's were always full of encouraging references that the Lord had given him. One reference I remember well, was from 2 Corinthians 4: 8,9: *"We are afflicted in every way, but not crushed; perplexed, but not despairing; persecuted, but not forsaken; struck down, but not destroyed."*

As the weeks passed, the Lord guided me to change lawyers. I prayed for the sum of $300 for the lawyer's fees and received a gift of $500 the next day. I made an appointment with the lawyer and the Lord undertook for me as I explained my reasons for the change, stating that the Lord gave me a certain amount of guidance, which I had to follow, and only He knew what was ahead. I was completely at peace and knew that my decision was correct. On the way home the scripture that the Lord gave me was from Colossians 3: 15. (G.N.B.): *"The peace that Christ gives you is to guide you in the decisions that you make, for it is to this peace that Christ has called you in the one body. And be thankful."* From that time on things began to move at a faster rate. We had been told that it would take up to a year for the appeal to reach the High Court; the new lawyers had a date set within a matter of weeks.

We were praying for a reduction of the length of sentence, or for a retrial. The next visiting time was approaching and I was praying about which of our four children I would take to visit their father (believing by faith that the Lord would make it possible). One week before this date, on 29 February, the case came to the High Court, and on that day the Lord made it possible for me to have our two older children with me, and the lawyers organised for my husband to be brought into court. He sat right in front of us for one and a half hours! He had lost a great deal of weight, between 40 and 50 pounds, but looked very well, indeed. Only the Lord could have arranged for us to be together in this way. My husband was even allowed to give his children a hug, which was totally unheard of.

During November 1987 our daughter had been selected to represent Zimbabwe in the United States for seven weeks. On the same course with her there had been a lady who was a judge in Harare. Our daughter was so impressed by this lady that she said to the Lord, "When Dad's case gets to the High Court, please can we have this judge?" When we rose to our feet as the judge entered the courtroom my daughter gasped; it was the same lady. The Lord had chosen the very best that He could for us. In previous weeks the date set for the hearing in the High Court had been changed and postponed time and time again, and we had continually told people that we must continue to praise the Lord, and wait for His choice. Now He really had done it. His choice of advocate was the highest, and we knew that the very best that could be done had been done for my husband.

The Lord had now worked out for me who I was to take to visit my husband - the two youngest. Once again He moved the mountains and they were allowed in. The 15 minutes was split among the three of us, but the children were only too happy to see their father, even if only through glass.

The High Court judgements were given on Wednesdays, and so we prayed and prayed from week to week for the judge and her decision.

Four days before the decision was given the song group was once again presenting their current programme to the church - "Victory in Jesus." Throughout the programme people testified to an area of victory in their lives, and once again God's power and presence was evident.

On the evening of the sixth week after the hearing I was standing at the sink, perfectly at peace after being told that the decision was to be given the next morning, when the words came to me unmistakeably, "Well done thou good and faithful servant." All the references we were given on that day were positive and encouraging. We knew that whatever the decision, it was the Lord's.

The next day the judgement was given. My husband was to be released immediately with a $5,000 fine, and the case was to be closed. I was at home when my friend phoned from the courtroom with the news. It was almost unbelievable; if the paperwork could be completed, my husband would be home by the end of the day. I shared the news with our daughter who was at home with the flu. My friend asked if I had $5,000 and I replied that I didn't, but I was sure I could get it.

I was told that if I couldn't, it was not a problem, as another friend was standing by willing to lend it to us. As I was unable to contact the person holding the pass book for the funds, I phoned our friend back, and he made the necessary arrangements for the money.

I then phoned some other friends with the news and the response was overwhelming; some simply "took off" and praised the Lord, others just burst into tears, but all were overjoyed. Within minutes telephone lines were buzzing all over, and all were rejoicing and praising God for His mighty intervention.

It took most of the day to complete the paperwork, and at 4 p.m., I went with a friend to bring my husband home from prison. He was released at 4:40 p.m., on the 13th April 1988. He had served five months and one day.

One other man had received a prison sentence with my husband, but he had been released on bail at the beginning of January and had only served seven weeks. My husband's bail had been refused, but it was largely the fact that he had served five months that swung the decision in his favour. The judge's remarks at the appeal judgement were that the original advocate had handled the case very poorly, that the so-called fraud was only a technical one, and that there was no moral blameworthiness to be attached to my husband. Our God does not make mistakes.

The children were overjoyed to have their father home and we praised and thanked the Lord together. Their prayers had been so positive and full of faith, and this was a wonderful answer to their months of prayers.

Within a couple of weeks of my husband's release, the $5,000 loan had been anonymously repaid. We never received a final account from the lawyers, but were simply told that also had been settled by two friends. It had been a figure of just under $3,000. The fund has only just been brought to an end, on the 1st July 1988. It ran for seven months and completely met all our needs.

Whilst in prison my husband prayed a lot about his work situation when released, as he knew that it would be difficult to find any employment. The Lord impressed upon him to "Work for yourself." Since his release, his thoughts have been confirmed; permanent work has been unavailable. However the Lord has a reason for everything and He opened up the way for my husband to purchase a computer, something he has been interested in for years, and he will work from home on accounts, word-processing, and however else the Lord leads.

He has just finished teaching a friend how to do word processing, as a very special "Thank You" as she was the one led by the Lord to start the fund.

I know that there is a great deal more to this testimony that could be written: many, many specific answers to prayers, and amazing areas of God's supply, but it has been written in a great hurry. We just pray that the Lord will make it possible for you to read what has been written and to share it with others for the sole purpose of uplifting the name of Jesus, and to bring glory to our great and mighty God.

Testimony Number Two
Beryl Shaw

During 1988 a testimony to God's power and provision for our family was written. For those who may not have read this testimony, it is the story describing how the Lord provided and undertook for our family when my husband was wrongfully accused and given a four year prison sentence. Due to the Lord's intervention, only five months of this sentence was actually served. At the retrial my husband was found not guilty and was released. Two references given at the time of the sentence were: "Truly, truly, I say to you, unless a grain of wheat falls into the earth and dies, it remains by itself alone, but if it dies it bears much fruit (John 12: 24), and from 1 Corinthians 15: 36: "You fool! That which you sow does not come to life unless it dies!"

From these verses we understood that the Lord was allowing my husband to die to himself and his old way of life, and that He was raising him up to a new life. We accepted that the way ahead was not going to be easy, and the testimony that follows is the story of how the Lord brought about the new life.

New Life In Him

A verse that will always be very special to me is Romans 8: 28, "And we know that God causes all things to work together for good to those who love God, to those who are called according to His purpose!" How very true is the wonderful promise contained in these words, that God will bring good out of all situations, good and bad alike.

Following my husband's release in April 1988 he experienced difficulty in obtaining employment. The way was opened to purchase a computer, which was to be used by him to teach word processing to provide an income. Unfortunately after only five months of use the computer was stolen from our home. Although other items stolen were covered by insurance the computer was not, with the result that we were still responsible for payment of the full amount of $27 000. The shock of the loss of the computer brought about a severe depression in my husband, he fell lower than any time previously and this continued for two months. Efforts to secure employment were to no avail. Immediately we started selling items from our home to make up the monthly payments of $561, plus our usual expenses, and school fees and bond. We started by clearing out items rarely used in our home, but as time went on more valuable items had to go: deep-freezer, radiogram, braais, electric drill, jewellery, glassware - the list was endless, and week by week and month by month, more and more items were sold to meet the payments. Selling our personal belongings was very hurtful indeed, but we were acutely aware that we dare not miss one computer payment: Five hundred and sixty one dollars was quite hard enough to find, it would have been almost impossible to raise over $1,100 in one go. I continually impressed this upon the children to help them understand the need to sell and keep up-to-date.

I was very aware that the Lord sets a time limit on everything, and explained as much to the children. Day by day I held on to God's promises: *"Fear not for I am with thee"*, (Isaiah 41: 10a.R.S.V.) *"I will never leave thee nor forsake thee."* (Hebrews 13: 5 K.J.V.) *"For I know the plans I have for you,"* says the Lord, *"plans for good and not for evil, to give you a future and a hope."* (Jeremiah 29: 11) I was continually aware that God was working out His perfect plan for our lives; it was not possible to see what He was doing, but I knew that He was rearranging our lives. Two very, very special and meaningful verses to me, written on a beautiful picture poster that one of the children had given me for Christmas, are from Isaiah 43: 18 and 19a, (R.S.V.) *"Remember not the former things, nor consider the things of old. Behold I am doing a new thing."* All along, I knew that the Lord was *"doing a new thing."* It was only standing on the promises of God daily that gave me the strength to go on.

Romans 5: 3,4: *"And not only this, but we exult in our tribulations, knowing that tribulation brings about perseverance, and perseverance, proven character, and proven character, hope."*

The lord was bringing about great changes in our lives and so I continued to thank and praise Him and continue on. Every day the Lord had fresh encouragement from His word. *"All discipline for the moment seems not to be joyful, but sorrowful; yet to those who have been trained by it afterwards it yields the peaceful fruit of righteousness. Therefore, strengthen the hands that are weak and the knees that are feeble."* (Hebrews 12: 11, 12) After two months the Lord intervened in our situation and raised up part-time work for my husband Mervyn; this was a great relief and the pressure of unemployment eased a little. Just before the computer was stolen, my husband was due to take on the Boys' Brigade books. Realising that he was now unable to undertake this work, the Boys' Brigade company decided to invest in a computer for their own use. However, this transaction took a period of five months as the item was purchased from overseas. Unfortunately on arrival it was discovered that a part had been damaged in transit and had to be returned for repair. Eventually the computer was operational and my husband had the use of it. It was now discovered that the doors to the teaching of word processing on a business basis had been closed, as the authorities did not encourage people teaching from home and we were no longer allowed to advertise. And so we continued to pray for full-time employment.

At this point I feel it important to share an agreement that Mervyn and I had made some 20 years ago when our children were very young and we were experiencing financial difficulties. We discussed the possibility of me returning to work, and considered the expenses that would be incurred; new clothes, extra petrol, nursery school fees, a worker for our home, more expensive cuts of meat, which could be prepared in less time. We weighed these against the value of me remaining at home with our children.

We agreed completely that my presence at home was of far greater value and importance than the small increase in finances we would experience, and we were far more prepared to forego the extra luxury items in our home than the welfare and security of our children. It was also clearly understood between us that Mervyn was far happier in answering his role as breadwinner in our home, and for my part I never wanted to be anywhere else. Our feelings have never changed in this matter and it was only as time progressed and no employment was forthcoming that I brought up the subject again. I was personally quite surprised at his response; he was most emphatic that I was of far greater value and help to our family and others in our home. It is true that I felt the same way, but had also felt that maybe I could be of some financial assistance. At this point the Lord revealed something of great importance to me: I was reminded of how difficult it had been over the weeks leaving Mervyn while I went for my weekly shopping; his face was so downcast and I had said to the children on more than one occasion, "Praise the Lord I do not go out every day, one day a week is quite bad enough for dad."

The continual unemployment and being unable to provide for his family was taxing him to the limit. The Lord showed me quite clearly that if Mervyn was to be raised up at all, then I must continue to submit and remain at home until His perfect timing, when He would bring it about in

His own way. For me to go out to work after Mervyn had experienced imprisonment, theft and unemployment, would result in almost total loss of self-respect. So we continued selling items from our house to make up the income needed, and thanked the Lord for the part-time work, which we were most grateful for. Eventually after two months of part-time employment, the Lord opened up another door most unexpectedly. As the minister of our church had left to take up another position, it was decided that Mervyn should be taken on as administrator. The position was mornings only with the added benefit of the use of the church car. How we praised the Lord for the car; it really was a blessing as our car had been in and out of the garage for nine months and could not be repaired due to the lack of spare parts. The following nine months spent at the church as administrator was a wonderful time of healing for Mervyn.

Many things needed attention, and as he involved himself in the life of the church the Lord gradually started to raise him up again and impart a sense of self worth. Once more he was a person who was needed and appreciated.

Opportunities arose for him to prepare sermons and conduct services; his messages were powerfully inspired by the Holy Spirit. Little by little the Lord was raising up a new person.

As the position was half-day only, we found it necessary to continue selling items from our house. This continued to be hard and hurtful, but enabled us to meet our monthly expenses. Approximately $1,000 had to found every month. Although this was distressing for all the members of the family, it was with great relief that we came to the end of each month with all expenses met.

The Lord continued to impress upon us the need to live one day at a time, and to be concerned for the needs of that day alone: Matthew 6: 34 states: *"Therefore do not be anxious for tomorrow, for tomorrow will care for itself. Each day has enough trouble of its own."* This was the basis of our prayers. During these months we experienced the most amazing answers to prayer, and the most extraordinary provision from the Lord. Top priority was given to meeting our monthly accounts, the first being the computer repayment as this was the largest. Each month when the salary was received all the money was paid out immediately. By faith we stood on God's promises that we must not worry about our daily needs for He knew them already and would provide. (Matthew 6: 31, 32). He says quite clearly, *"But seek first His Kingdom and His righteousness;*

and all these things shall be added to you" (Matthew 6: 33). We knew that unpaid accounts would not be glorifying to the Lord and therefore must be met. As we continued to step out in faith the Lord continued to provide for our needs, after the computer repayment came the bond repayment. To ensure a roof over our heads was of utmost importance! Stop orders for insurances and medical aid payments were also necessities; each account was met one by one. We concerned ourselves with the immediate needs. Even as I write this, some two years later, I praise God for the way in which He impressed upon us so very strongly the need to live one day at a time, and realise that had we dwelt upon the enormity of our situation, the money owed on the computer and the monthly accounts, it would surely have crushed us. As we continued to use the finances that came into our home, by one means or another, to pay our accounts, the Lord in all His faithfulness, provided our daily food.

As I am writing this I read from my diary dated 1-9-89: "Praise the Lord, meat and groceries from Patty", (Friends names changed) 4-9-89: "Praise the Lord a gift of $50 via our daughter's office, perfect timing before shopping tomorrow." 6-9-89: *"Praise the Lord, eggs and vegetables from Janet and juice from Patty."*

The Lord was also sensitive toward Mervyn and me regarding time out together: on the 7-9-89 we were absolutely thrilled to receive two complimentary tickets to the theatre; to be able to relax and thoroughly enjoy the show "Camelot" amid our difficult circumstances was a true blessing from the Lord and we praised Him for our friend who had blessed us with this special gift.

Day by day we continually prayed for our needs and at one stage were praying for the sum of $40 for our son's art fees. I was led to turn out some old clothes. The entry in my diary reads: "Praise the Lord, $50 received from clothes, will pay Greg's art fees ($40)." Greg resumed his art classes the next day, after a holiday break of three weeks. We praised the Lord that he was able to take his fees with him.

His perfect timing never ceased to amaze us. I am in the habit of shopping on a Tuesday, and to avoid unnecessary disruption I continued with my routine. Even when I had no money to shop with, I dressed for town and went out expecting the Lord to provide. He never let me down. One morning as I was leaving the house empty-handed, our daughter handed me a bag of clothes stating that I might be able to get something for them. (She was unaware that I had no money.) I was also planning to visit my mother-in-law. In my diary I have written on the 12-9-89: "Praise the Lord, $35 received from clothes and $10 fuel money from Janet. Went shopping."

Most Tuesday mornings I was in the habit of collecting a vegetable list for the market from a friend's letter box, and on one particular morning the note enclosed read, "$10 for me and $10 for you." I would like to share at this point that this particular friend also trusts the Lord for her daily needs and has the very special gift of giving; it is through this channel of love that the Lord provides for her and her family.

One area of the Lord's provision, on the surface, may appear small and insignificant, it is the area of those "little things" that help to make life more pleasant and comfortable; I personally see them as "Mighty miracles." One morning as I was standing at the kitchen sink I had a need for some green washing soap, and I said to the Lord, "You know, Lord, I could really do with some green soap right now". Within five minutes the son of a friend called to have his time of piano practise, and he handed me a small brown paper packet from his mother. You can guess what was in it - a square of green soap!! I was reminded that the Lord provides just what we need for our daily use; He knew that I didn't need a whole bar, but just one square.

There was also another occasion which will always remain vividly in my mind: One evening I had such a craving for a sweet! I searched the kitchen cupboards, even running my fingers along the inside edges in the hope of finding one, but to no avail. I considered asking one of our sons to go to the local cafe to buy a small packet (it was quite a craving, and we hadn't had sweets for months) but then thought better of it, as the only money I had in the house was for milk the next day. I then asked our son, Kevin, to deliver a small packet of "goodies" to a friend. A little later as I passed through the kitchen I saw a packet of sweets on the cupboard. I called Kevin and asked him where they had come from; did he go to the cafe? (even though he was not aware of my desire for a sweet). His reply was, "No. When I delivered your packet, I was given these." My friend shared with me later that she had been given two packets of sweets that day, and that one was obviously for someone else. Through this "little" incident the Lord spoke most powerfully to me. He showed me how much He cared for me, how much I meant to Him, and just how incredibly He knew our every need and desire. I have only to think back on this incident alone to be reminded that He knows every detail of our lives, and that He most graciously provides. "But seek first His kingdom, and His righteousness; and all these things shall be added to you."

One Tuesday, on 30/1/90, with less than $10 for groceries, it was only possible to buy the absolute essentials for the day. I praised the Lord, knowing that He knew our needs. The knowledge that He would provide had become a way of life, but I was not prepared for the overwhelming way in which He was about to provide for us. During the course of the afternoon a friend delivered the most enormous box of groceries, plus an envelope containing the sum of $457. It was a gift from the members of another congregation. Apparently, a friend, a member of this particular congregation, had felt led to share our situation during a time of fellowship two days before. The Lord had moved upon the hearts of the members, and this was the result. His perfect timing left us in sheer amazement. At this very time we had been praying for the sum of $300 for the car insurance, and $100 for dentist's fees!

The following Tuesday, (6/2/90), yet another amazing thing happened. Once again I was very short of grocery money, and bought only the day's needs. During the course of the afternoon, a lady whom I had only met on three or four occasions, accompanied by her son, delivered two large boxes of groceries. I was absolutely amazed. I was even more amazed, and deeply touched, when I learned that they had been left to us by my visitor's late mother-in-law, who had recently gone to be with the Lord. That dearest lady, whose deep faith had been the greatest encouragement and inspiration to me over the years, had continued to be the sweetest blessing, even after she had died.

If it were not for the fact that I have taken the third incident from my diary on Tuesday 13/2/90, I would forgive you for not believing me. Once again I had only a very limited amount of grocery money, and I quote from my diary: "Praise the Lord - yet another huge gift of groceries. From someone in Nancy's Bible Study Group, His usual perfect timing."

I feel that it is necessary to share with you that very few people were aware that Tuesday was my shopping day. For three consecutive weeks the Lord had provided over and above.

And so this way of life continued on for approximately one and a half years, and throughout this time a figure of $1,000 was made up every month. The money came from many different sources - the sale of clothes, household and personal items, medical aid refunds, gifts, - the list was endless.

At one point, when the situation was very serious indeed, and we were praying for the usual large amounts needed at the beginning of one month, we quite unexpectedly received notice that my father's house had been sold, and we had been left a sum of money. My father is retired and lives in Australia. He shared with me in a recent letter that some years ago he felt that one day the money might be useful "for a rainy day." Praise God that both He and my father had made provision for us years in advance. As we continued to pay our accounts, the Lord continued to provide day by day: meat, vegetables, fuel money, milk tokens and many other items. Apart from the special treat of the visit to the theatre, on more than one occasion Mervyn and I received envelopes containing gifts of money with an enclosed message, "Dinner for two, and a film afterwards". Over the months we have come to understand clearly that it is most important for gifts of money received in this way to be used as specified.

Apart from the fact that it is a loving gesture from friends, and they would be very hurt to discover that the money had been used in a different way, we also accepted that they were simply being used as channels of God's love and concern for our welfare. Living as we were, continually selling our personal belongings, and praying constantly for our every need became, at times, very tiring, and the Lord in His graciousness knew that we needed encouragement and a break.

There were many other pressures, too. Our three sons, Kevin, Gregory and Craig are continually using their bicycles as their only mode of transport to and from work and lessons, and they ride hundreds of kilometres every week.

Punctures are a very regular occurrence due to broken glass on our roads, and every night, without fail, someone is mending a puncture. Due to lack of finances it simply was not possible to replace tyres and tubes, which were very often not available anyway; so they had to repair them the best way they could. I remember one evening watching Greg sewing up the outside of his tyre with fishing line! Praise the Lord it held until it could be replaced later.

Then we had a run of thefts. We had just received our Mercedes back from the garage when, one night, it was broken into and the radio/tape player was slashed out with a knife. Further damage was also done when the electric wiring was pulled out from under the dashboard, presumably in an effort to start the car. Sadly, we were unable to claim from the insurance company, as this would have meant losing our "No Claims Bonus", and we would not have been able to afford the renewal premiums due very shortly. The church car also suffered loss: three times in succession the side lights and indicators were stolen, and one night the spare wheel was taken. On another occasion the jack was stolen from the Mercedes. (Sometimes we were quite grateful that our car spent half its life at the garage - its "second home" we used to call it.) Both cars by now had alarms fitted, and every night for weeks on end these were sounding off. A full night's sleep was unheard of.

At five-o'-clock one morning as I was cleaning the kitchen I looked out of the open door, and there I saw the Mercedes standing minus its front headlamps. By this stage I did not even know how to share the news with Mervyn, but he had to be told. You can just imagine how it affected him; to replace the headlamps would cost about $1,000 each. Immediately he telephoned the police station, and was informed that someone had been caught with stolen property, amongst which was a set of headlamps. He was asked if he would go and identify them as his property.

As the church car was at this point undergoing repairs the only transport available was a bicycle, and so he went on that. I feel the story Mervyn was told at the police station is worth repeating; it certainly added a little humour to the situation. The previous evening a man in our area awoke during the night and saw from his window the wheels being removed from his car. He telephoned the police station, who in turn called their vehicle by radio, instructing it to return to the station. The police vehicle returned to the station, and as it turned into the drive a tyre blew out.

Their spare wheel had been stolen sometime in the past, and so another station in the area was contacted, and a vehicle was despatched to the given address. As this vehicle approached the house where the incident had happened, the thieves attempted to escape but the driver panicked and stalled their car. The driver fled, but after a tussle the police apprehended the three remaining persons.

The items recovered that night from this incident included four wheels and tyres, three complete headlamp and radiator grill assemblies from different makes of cars, and our headlamps! We certainly praised the Lord for their recovery.

At no point throughout all these events did I ever doubt that the Lord was with us and in control. I realised that He had a plan and a purpose for all that was taking place in our lives. I was reminded continually that He sets a time limit on all things, and that He would not overstep that limit. One of the most encouraging things that he continually impressed upon me through His word was that at the end of it there would be a time of blessing.

However, due to pressures and tiredness my health was feeling the strain. In addition to the things I have shared I had to contend with broken household appliances, one being a washing machine that persisted in flooding the laundry floor. It was not possible to have the items repaired, as funds were not available, and for anyone doing their own housework, broken appliances are very wearing indeed. At one stage I turned to the Lord in desperation, asking him to intervene. The way in which He moved completely staggered me. On the same day I received a phone call from a friend in Scotland with whom I had not had contact for many months. The Lord had laid a burden for my welfare on her heart, and she phoned to say that I must read Ephesians 6, verses 10 to 18, three times each day for one week. This was without me sharing anything with her, and the intervention was incredible.

Through the reading of these verses the Lord revealed to me that it was my mind that was under the severest attack. Praise God that through the week He ministered to me and lifted me above the situation. I saw clearly that I had been fighting the devil himself through the thoughts he had placed in my mind, and through the self pity that had crept in. I confessed my sins to the Lord, took hold of the word of God, and came up against the devil. Praise God for the victory in his word, "Submit therefore to God. Resist the devil and he will flee from you." (James 4: 7)

Once again I was left in awe of our great and loving God to think that He had laid my burden on the heart of a friend 10,000 kilometres away, and how I praised Him for her obedience. To this day I do not think she realises to what extent the Lord had used her.

Once again His word came to me powerfully, *"In this you greatly rejoice, even though now for a little while, if necessary, you have been distressed by various trials, that the proof of your faith, being more precious than gold which is perishable, even though tested by fire, may be found to result in praise and glory and honour at the revelation of Jesus Christ."* (1 Peter 1:6, 7)

As I praised the Lord He began to reveal new things to me. One thing that came to me very strongly was that He had allowed us to lose everything; employment, finances and worldly goods, because He was setting us on a new course, teaching us from scratch, that it was to be "a new life."

I had prayed in previous months that he would teach us to be better stewards of His resources. We had for many years been in the habit of giving and helping others, and now He was teaching us how to be more effectual in financial matters. He was teaching us a new value of money.

Every month we had a "Monthly Prayer list" in our kitchen, and the whole family prayed for specific items - bicycle tyres and tubes, brake cables, school suitcase, examination fees, washing machine repairs, clothes, watch battery, tackies, kettle element - the lists were endless. As the Lord provided, the items were crossed off, and the date written in. By the end of each month the needs had been supplied.

Apart from praying for these daily needs, our thoughts were also centred on something far greater. In previous years our daughter Karen and our son Kevin, had attended Girls' and Boys' Brigades Camps in other countries, and now, Gregory, our third child, had the opportunity of attending a camp in Australia at the end of the year (1989).

In our circumstances many people might have thought the idea quite out of the question, but we had known for two years that it was quite correct for Greg to attend the camp, and that it was totally in the Lord's will.

With His help it became possible for us to raise over $4,000 for Gregory alone and he attended the camp. Funds were actually raised for about 20 boys and officers, and the trip included England, Singapore and Australia. Apart from the wonderful experience of the camp, Greg was also blessed with a visit to his Grandfather and other relatives in Australia and England, some of whom he had not met before.

Praise God again for His word, *"... all things are possible to him who believes,"* (Mark 9: 23b). *"Delight yourself in the Lord and He will give you the desires of your heart."* (Psalms 37: 4)

We experienced the "high times" and also the "low times", and one of my lowest times was when we had virtually come to the end of things in our home that could be sold. All the smaller items had gone - guitar tuner, electric drill, electric shavers, ornaments - the only thing that could now help us through was my beautiful 12-string Yamaha guitar, a gift from my husband three years before. I experienced something similar to that of other Christians I had read of - how the Lord gives the most incredible strength to handle painful situations, and then following the victory, the sinking weakness as we are faced with the reality of the situation.

However, the Lord continued to undertake for me and as I used Greg's guitar to lead a singing group in a Christmas programme that very afternoon, I was aware of His peace and presence.

We had now moved in to 1990, and after Mervyn had been working as the church administrator for nine months our new minister arrived. We had once again been praying for employment, and two days before his arrival, the Lord opened the doors for mornings only employment for Mervyn, for which we were very grateful. By this time I had come to realise that a position Mervyn was happy in was administrative, and involving computer work.

So, when he went for the interview I specifically prayed that a computer would be available for him; and that if the firm did not have one the Lord would direct them to purchase one!

(At the time of the interview we did not even know what the position was and what was entailed.)

The position was an administrative one, and there was a small lap-top computer he could use. Within a few weeks the need became evident for a larger one, and so a new one was bought.

At this time our car was back in the garage, and naturally the minister had to have the use of the church car, so transport was once again under prayer. I was utterly amazed when after only a short time Mervyn was offered the use of a company car; it took me a full 24 hours to take in this fantastic answer to prayer.

Our situation was improving tremendously, but we were still a few hundred dollars short each month. I knew that the Lord could provide additional finances, but for some reason was withholding them at this time. Obviously He wanted to teach us more, and the fault had to be on our side, and that more adjustment was needed in our lives.

I do not question the Lord's ways, I only ask Him to help me to see what He wants to teach me. The verse He gave me was from Psalms 25 verses 8 and 9: *"Good and upright is the Lord; therefore He instructs sinners in the way. He leads the humble in justice, and He teaches the humble His way."* I praised Him for assuring me that He would teach us and show us His way.

It is a wonderful thing to know that when we are really searching seriously for God's help and direction He does show us the way. "And you will seek Me and find Me, when you search for Me with all your heart. And I will be found by you ..." (Jeremiah 29: 13,14a)

At this time Kevin was attending some Christian meetings being held in town, and spoke very highly of the visiting speaker. He shared many of the deep insights with us, one of them being the need to tithe. For some length of time after Mervyn had become unemployed we had continued this practise.

However, as time went on and we found that we were receiving the exact amounts of money we had been praying for, we were faced with the decision of making the full payment of an account, or only part of it. After discussion we decided that we should pay the full amount so, sadly, tithing fell away for almost a year. Praise the Lord the children continued tithing their personal incomes for which I was most grateful. Some few weeks before this, He had already spoken to me through a very special friend. The friend had simply shared very excitedly her own personal experience in this area, and how the Lord had blessed and prospered her family.

We understood that the Christian meetings had come to an end, and we were disappointed. Then we heard that one more was to be held at a Christian Businessmen's lunch, and I prayed about the possibility of Mervyn attending. My feelings are that when we are sick we visit a doctor, and if spiritual help is needed we go to a man of God. I felt very strongly that this was the person the Lord had raised up in our particular situation. Mervyn received an invitation to the luncheon, and although we did not have the funds for him to attend, he went off trusting the Lord.

He did actually take some money with him that had been set aside for another need, but we felt very strongly that our spiritual lives were of the utmost importance at this stage. I did, however, pray that he would not have to use the money. Praise the Lord, a friend very kindly stood him to the lunch.

The two main areas that struck home to Mervyn in the talk were those of "Tithing" and "Accepting responsibility for mistakes and failures." Together, and individually, we prayed through these areas.

The Lord impressed upon me the need to increase my giving in any way I could - time, groceries, and any other way He showed me. I came to realise that the flow of groceries into our home had decreased, and realised at the same time that I had not been giving out as much as I used to. We had so very little, but no matter how small, I started giving away a portion; a tiny amount of margarine, two or three eggs, a few beans. Every time I visited someone or had a caller, I gave. And, it was not my imagination when I noticed that the flow into our home started increasing - it was miraculously noticeable. It goes without saying that Mervyn and I had once again been thoroughly convicted on the need to practise tithing, and it was with the greatest joy that we presented our first, very special, tithe again to the Lord at the first opportunity given. It was then that the Lord showed me the wonderful miracle He had performed: we were now giving with very thankful and joyful hearts, and I had new insight to His word, *"for God loves a cheerful giver."* (2 Corinthians 9: 7b) In the past we had tithed happily, but it was not really an effort as the Lord had blessed us with a good income, and we were simply being obedient to His word (Malachi 3: 10).

As a result of our past year with all its ups and downs, and feelings of guilt over not giving as we felt we should, He had brought about the most wonderful changes within us. Now it was the greatest privilege to give back to Him just a very small portion of what already, rightfully, belonged to Him.

It was now June 1990, and we were expecting visitors from overseas. I had been very concerned about the severe lack in our home of linen, crockery, and of course the financial aspect; and all had been committed to the Lord. As the time grew closer I realised that it was not going to be possible to replace these items, and I felt that I might have to borrow. My prayers turned in this direction, and within a very short space of time I had friends offering all manner of things. I gratefully accepted offers of bed linen, and approached a friend about the possibility of borrowing beds. They were lent most willingly, complete with even more linen! I actually returned some of it to a friend, as the need had been more than met. As an added blessing we were given a large gift of meat, which was more than adequate for our needs.

I continued to pray for bathroom curtains, and the night before our visitors arrived I was given two most beautiful lace curtains, one of which was made into some very suitable bathroom curtains. During the previous week the Lord had shown me that some of the items I had prayed for were unnecessary- extra crockery and glassware that was not really needed. During the duration of our friends' stay the Lord continued to provide our daily needs in the same way that he had done over the past year. It was yet another time of learning and growth for our family.

Shortly after this, as I continued to search for the Lord's ways, He convicted me in the area of waste. Numerous lights left on in the evening, unnecessary loads of washing resulting in excessive quantities of washing powder, water and electricity being used. I was also in the habit of switching on the stove long before it was required. It did not help the situation when I realised that the oven thermostat was faulty, which meant that the oven was permanently on at a low temperature. I began to switch the stove off at the main wall switch. I had been convicted of the need to reduce the monthly electricity and water account. Two months later I was absolutely thrilled at the result; the account had been reduced by 25 per cent. I had also been convicted on the need to make and sell lemon curd. It was amazing how the Lord used this small income to help us.

We were most grateful for Mervyn's employment, and the use of the car, but during the course of July the only remaining item that I felt could be sold to keep our family debt- free was my piano. I finally faced the situation that I had been avoiding, the distinct possibility of having to part with it. The piano had been given to me as a very special gift by a young woman who had attended a youth group, which Mervyn and I had led in previous years. At the time it had been a wonderful answer to prayer and had always been used for the Lord's work.

I am afraid that this was more than I could handle, and I completely broke, and told the Lord that I could not part with it; and that I honestly did not think that this was His will, although we could not go on for another month as we were.

Once again our car had been repaired and returned to us, but for some months now it had been incurring high costs in garage charges, and we had come to realise that it had to be sold in an effort to clear the account. It was also a fact that we could no longer afford to run the Mercedes and keep up the computer payments. We felt that it might be possible to clear the outstanding balance on the computer by selling the car, and so we started advertising.

Although our situation looked bleak, when I looked back over the last one and a half years I was absolutely amazed that we had actually kept going for so long.

The Lord's provision and intervention had been quite miraculous, and I felt that it should be shared with others. I started praying for this opportunity. I also had the very distinct feeling that the Lord was about to intervene mightily in some way, and had shared this with the family. A friend had also confirmed this thought, and I was personally feeling very excited about it.

Within a week of starting to pray, I had a phone call from a friend who was a member of the church that had supported us previously. He asked if I would pray about the possibility of going to share with their fellowship. I laughed and explained that I had already prayed about it, and that I was willing to go. The date was set for two weeks ahead, Sunday the 22nd of July.

We witnessed as a family, and the Lord undertook for us. Mervyn shared that he felt it possible that an area of pride in his life had been one of the contributing factors to the problems our family was experiencing. Kevin's talk covered the way in which the Lord teaches us through our own difficult circumstances to care and be concerned for other members in the body of Christ; and Karen brought out the way in which the Lord had drawn us closer together as a family, through working together. Two verses that had meant a great deal to her at the time are from Proverbs 15: verses 16 and 17. "Better is a little with the fear of the Lord, than great treasure and turmoil with trouble." And, "Better is a dish of vegetables where love is than a fattened ox and hatred with it." At the end of the evening a "love offering" was taken and given to us consisting of $172. We truly praised the Lord.

Following the evening of sharing we received several anonymous gifts of money, for which we were very, very grateful. Each gift met a specific need.

Four days later Mervyn phoned from the office to say he had been offered full-time employment. He was so overwhelmed he could hardly speak. At the end of the day we joined together as a family in thanking and praising the Lord. On Wednesday 1st August, Mervyn returned to full-time employment for the first time in four years, and the next day I was given the most wonderful promise from God's word; from Jeremiah 32, verse 42 I read *"For thus says the Lord, 'Just as I brought all this great disaster on this people, so am I going to bring on them all the good that I am promising them.'"*

The month of August was a most incredible one. We had to go yet another month until our first full salary. Throughout the whole of the month the Lord provided unbelievably, but what he did impress upon me very strongly was the absolute need to keep on giving. "Give, and it will be given to you; good measure, pressed down, shaken together, running over they will pour into your lap. For by your standard of measure it will be measured to you in return." (Luke 6: 38) I gave one lettuce, and received three in return; of these, I gave two and got back six; I gave four eggs and was given six; I gave away a small piece of meat and on the next day received a chicken! One important lesson I learned was that if we give food, we receive food; if we give money, we will receive money, which was a very exciting insight. And so we came to the end of August, and the Lord had once again undertaken for us.

During the past weeks we had continually advertised the car for sale, and had not been able to understand why it had not gone. At the start we had not had much of an idea of a realistic figure, and so asked a mechanic who suggested about $13,000. We were unsure, but the balance outstanding on the computer was approximately $13,000 , and the garage account was just over three thousand. We advertised, inviting offers, and having learned that for our model the price should be about $15,000 to $16,000 decided to negotiate around that value. Week by week we continued to advertise and asked for offers, but to no avail.

We then advertised stating our price, but still had no success. One or two people offered much lower figures, which we considered accepting, although we felt that there would be little point in selling the car if the amount realised did not cover our needs. However, we were feeling really despondent and had made the decision to drop the figure to $13,000 the next week. On Sunday, 26 August, we visited friends for tea, and spoke about the car. Our friend said our price was too low!! People would think that a Mercedes offered at $15,000 or $16,000 must have something wrong with it - we must put the price up, as we could always drop it. (Although these figures may seem unreasonable, at this period in Zimbabwe's history inflation was escalating at an alarming rate. It was heading towards the hyper-inflation which would later affect the country with disastrous results).

On Wednesday, 29 August, I had a phone call from a friend in Botswana; she had phoned for a prayer request, but also went on to say, "Beryl, I don't know what you are asking for your car, but every time I pray about it I feel so uneasy, and feel that I must tell you that your price is too low, and that you must put it up!" The following week we advertised the car at $20,000 , and on Monday, 3 September the car sold for $15,700, the amount needed to clear the garage account and the outstanding balance on the computer. What a mighty God we serve!

It is now five years since Mervyn was first suspended, and as a family we have lost a great deal in terms of worldly goods, but I feel that what we have gained spiritually far outweighs this. Above all else, the Lord has raised Mervyn up, and has equipped him not only for His service, but also for a better position in the secular world. He has now been employed on a full-time basis for eight months.

For our family it has been a time of rebuilding and replacing. We have continued to work hard in our home and garden, and the Lord is blessing the fruit of our labours.

In November 1990 our daughter Karen won a return airfare to London at a secretary's conference. It was simply a draw for the lucky candidate number. She had actually said at the start of the conference, "Lord, if I win that ticket I'm giving it to Mum!" For many years Karen had wanted to give me the gift of a trip overseas, and this has made it possible. It took a great while for me to take in the enormity of this gift, and I had to be sure I was in the Lord's will by accepting it. He had provided the ticket, and I would have to trust Him to provide my finances and personal needs.

Since leaving England 30 years ago I have not returned, and in the past years I have had a very strong desire to go back for a visit. I have three sisters there, and it will be the first time in over 30 years that all four sisters will be in England together.

Karen had already planned to visit England, and so we will be leaving together in one week's time, on the 29 March, 1991. I will be going for one month and Karen for seven. I am feeling very excited, and the Lord is providing for my needs. We are most grateful, and praise God for our wonderful friends and family who have supported and encouraged us for so long now, and we pray that He will bless each one abundantly.

As I have reread my diary, and written this testimony, I have been reminded of the Lord's presence with our family over the past five years. And it is with total conviction that I say that I would not have had the strength to continue on without His constant encouragement and reassurance through His word, day by day. To God be all the glory.

I end this testimony with two very special promises: The first from Philippians 4: 19, *"And my God shall supply all your needs according to His riches in glory in Christ Jesus,"* and the second, Ephesians 3: 20, 21, "Now to Him who is able to do exceeding abundantly beyond all that we ask or think, according to the power that works within us, to Him be glory in the church and in Christ Jesus to all generations for ever and ever. Amen."

Beryl Shaw

CHAPTER FOURTEEN

Revelations in Prayer

"Now there are varieties of gifts, but the same Spirit. And there are varieties of ministries, and the same Lord."
1 Corinthians 12: 4, 5.

Life at home now became extremely busy as the number of people coming for prayer increased daily. It was truly amazing what the Lord was doing in people's lives.

I am deeply grateful to a minister who once gave me this wise word of advice. He said, "Whenever people come to you for help, get them into God's presence as quickly as possible. Go to God in prayer." He explained to me that *we* don't have all the answers to the problems that people have, but God does.

The first real insight I had pertaining to this truth was exciting and encouraging. One morning a young man came to me with a problem and asked for my advice. I explained that I didn't have the answer to the problem, but that we'd pray about it together. We had not long been in prayer when the young man excitedly said, "I know what I must do," and went on to explain to me how he could go about sorting the problem out. He thanked me most profusely for my help, but I explained to him that it had not been me that had given him the solution, but God.

It used to concern me that people came to me with serious problems and expected me to have the answers, which I did not have. It was a fact that numerous people had come for prayer over the years and God had been overwhelmingly gracious in meeting their needs. However, as the number of people increased and their needs appeared to be greater, I had felt increasingly inadequate. I continually reminded myself that the work was God's and that I was just His instrument. The realisation and acceptance of the fact that I *did not* have all the answers, but that God did, was of the utmost importance to me. As the years passed, this knowledge increased and strengthened my faith to continue on in His work. I was further encouraged through the manifestation of the gifts, which the Lord bestows upon us for ministry.

I remember feeling *extremely* threatened one morning when a young man, who I'll call Simon, arrived for ministry. I had never met him before. All the while he was explaining his problems to me as he paced the room before me, which I found somewhat unnerving. From his conversation I quickly perceived that he was a very intellectual person. I also gained the impression that he was not really expecting to receive much help from the ministry. While listening to him I was continually sending up arrow prayers to the Lord for help because I was beginning to feel most inadequate to cope with this young man.

Eventually we went to prayer. Simon's need for healing of past memories was immense and so I commenced with a prayer of inner healing. I had encouraged him to stop me at any point, if he felt that he would like to share something specific that the Lord had brought to his attention. I think what followed was an amazement to both of us. Throughout the prayer the Lord gave me particular visions pertaining to Simon's childhood, simple things, including the scene of a rowing boat on a lake with an elderly man in it. Another was of an entrance hall of a house with two staircases leading upwards, one straight and the other curved. As I described the visions to Simon one by one, he promptly confirmed what I was describing and immediately gave an explanation. He gave the location and the circumstances surrounding his visits to these particular places. It was obvious, from his explanations, that the Lord was highlighting the most painful experiences from Simon's childhood, the very areas that the Lord desired to heal.

At one point I received a truly amazing vision of torrents of water thundering over an enormous waterfall. I was acutely aware of the powerful movement of the water cascading over the high precipice. I described to Simon what I saw and was experiencing. I explained "that the Lord was setting him free from past hurts, and was washing away the pain of childhood memories, and that out of his life would flow rivers of living water." Whereupon he laughed and said, "I know exactly what you are describing, I'm not going to tell you about it now, but when I come back next week I will show you."

After we had been at prayer for approximately an hour and a half, I brought our time to a close. It was quite obvious that the Lord had performed a mighty work in Simon's life, and he was full of amazement and praise to God for what had taken place. We made an appointment to meet again the following week.

Obviously I was intrigued to know what it was that Simon wanted to show me. Something pertaining to the vision had clearly caused him great excitement. When he returned a week later he handed me a roll of thick paper, measuring 30 x 40 centimetres in size. I unrolled the paper, and, written in beautiful calligraphy, was a poem. The whole presentation was delightful to look at. I started to read the poem and as I read I became more and more amazed at what was unravelling before me. The writing, which was titled, "Psalm of Souls," and commenced with the words, "Lord, I am only a dry lake," was actually a most beautiful and moving prayer. From the depths of his heart Simon had poured out his soul to the Lord, beseeching Him to renew his life and overflow him by the power of the Holy Spirit.

Simon explained to me that it was this poem that he had recalled while I was describing the vision, and that the vision that had come to him when writing the poem, had now been fulfilled. I was even more amazed when he went on to explain that he had written the poem many years before at high school in South Africa, and had won second place in a creative writing competition. (This is verified on the back of the paper.) He now wanted to give the work to me. I, of course, did not feel that I could accept such a special gift, but Simon insisted, saying, that, "Years before he had wanted to give it to a lady, but that she would not take it, so he had said to the Lord, 'The next person that You show me to give it to, I will.'" And went on to say, "And it's you. So you *must* take it." In the light of this I could not refuse. I treasure the work to this day.

Beryl Shaw

CHAPTER FIFTEEN

Set Free to Serve

Jesus therefore was saying to those Jews who had believed Him, "If you abide in My word, then you are truly disciples of Mine; and you shall know the truth, and the truth shall make you free." John 8: 31,32.

One Sunday morning I was on door duty at the church, greeting people for the morning worship. A dear friend, Steph, came in, and as I welcomed her I was surprised to see that her usual cheery face was very downcast. When I greeted her she burst into tears and explained that she was suffering from excruciating pain in her back. She had attended medical practitioners during the week, but no amount of treatment had helped to relieve the pain. She requested prayer following the service. At the close of the service I asked Mervyn and two other friends to join me in prayer for our friend. We gathered around her and started interceding, asking the Lord to heal her back and relieve the pain. I had my hand resting very lightly on Steph's back, when suddenly she jumped and let out a cry. I immediately asked her if I had been resting my hand on her too heavily, (although I did not think this was the case), and I asked her what she had felt. As she described the sensation that she had just experienced, and the fact that the pain and discomfort had immediately left her, we realised that, there and then, the Lord had released His healing power into her back and had restored it to health and strength. Judging by the way Steph described it, He "Had put back into place whatever was out!" She was now completely free from pain and discomfort.

It was evident that God was causing a mighty outpouring of His Holy Spirit to fall upon the believers. As word spread about the work that He was doing in the lives of people, the numbers requesting ministry increased, particularly amongst those suffering depression. As the months went on I began to feel the strain of repeating the same words over and over. I took my concerns to the Lord in prayer, laying it all before Him. I also requested prayer from friends. In my prayers I remember saying to the Lord, "I can't stop because the needs are so great, but I don't know how I can continue with the number of people coming." The answer that came to me was, "Write it down." The Lord was directing me to write down the things that people needed to know. This was to be a simple explanation of the underlying problems facing Christians, and the steps to follow to gain healing and control over their lives. He showed me that it would simplify the ministry as it would lift the burden of repeating myself. Instead, I could just pass a book to people. With the information at their fingertips, they would be in a position to refer to it as and when needed.

I took up pen and paper and immediately set about writing. A few weeks later two small books had been written and printed. The first was called, *Fight for Your Life*, and the second, *Victory in Jesus.*

From my experience of ministering to those suffering from depression I came to realise that, for them, it really was a fight for their sanity. Hence the name, Fight for Your Life, which is an introduction to spiritual warfare, bearing in mind that people were not involved in a physical fight, but a spiritual one, as we are told in Ephesians 6: 12. Victory in Jesus was a sequel to the first book and pertains to rising above the difficulties people face in their daily lives.

At a later stage a third book entitled *Healing Streams* was compiled and was of comfort to those in need. And finally I wrote *Renewal of the Mind.* The books were readily accepted and widely distributed. The information contained in them has proved to be of great help to those in need, besides being a welcome asset to the ministry.

For many years I had the privilege of working very closely with Sue in the Inner Healing and Deliverance ministry. Sue was a good and faithful friend and held the position of Session Clerk in the Hatfield Presbyterian

Church. Throughout the difficult years the Lord sent many people to us for His healing touch, and it was exciting and encouraging to witness lives being unbound and set free, relationships being restored and strengthened, and people receiving new vision and hope for their lives. We can testify to these facts, and know without a doubt that we serve a mighty God, through whom all things are possible.

Eventually this ministry was placed under the headship of the church as a recognised organisation within the Hatfield Presbyterian Church, under the name of "Life and Wholeness." This name was confirmed through God's word as given in Proverbs 4: 20 – 22, *"My son, give attention to my words; incline your ear to my sayings. Do not let them depart from your sight; keep them in the midst of your heart. For they are life to those who find them, and health to all their whole body."*

The testimonies that follow were written personally by two individual ladies who came for ministry. Both had the joy of discovering the power in the written word, and were given the strength to overcome the debilitating effects of depression.

"MY FIGHT FOR SANITY"
Anonymous

I arrived in Salisbury from South Africa with my parents at the age of two. I grew up in a fairly poor home, like a number of us, but with many advantages of living in this beautiful country in the 1940s and 1950s. I was the oldest of three children, having two younger brothers. There were insecurities in my life as a child; my parents fought a lot, often speaking of divorce. I had to stay alone in the dark, and was terrified of being alone, evil spirits and other imaginings, so I didn't sleep well, and this has remained the pattern of my life. I became rebellious at senior school. I was lonely, insecure and had very little self-confidence: my schoolwork suffered severely and I felt a hopeless failure, as I had no qualifications.

I met my husband when I was 19 years old. He was such fun to be with, handsome, confident and charming. We had a wonderful, whirlwind courtship and got married a year later, when I was 20. We had a very beautiful, loving marriage and he built up my self-confidence and I felt loved and secure. We had three lovely children, a beautiful home, and I had everything a woman could want. Yet I had a longing to be healed, for a preacher to lay his hands on my head. I did not know who to go to, or why I felt like this, and started searching for the truth and I continued like this for some years. I felt very guilty about my sinful thoughts. One day a friend told me that there was power in the name of Jesus, and to believe that the Bible is God's word, and that He would answer many questions *after* and not *before* I believed. I lay on the couch one Sunday when I was alone and called on the name of Jesus, saying I needed Him in my life, if He was really there, and asking Him to forgive me, a lousy rotten sinner. Immediately I heard a sound like rushing water going into me, especially in my ears and, as I learned later, was filled with the Holy Spirit. At the time I did not know what was happening. I was overwhelmed and excited and as a result of my experience I joined my friend's church in 1970. My husband and the children followed and we had four blissful, happy years, the happiest in my life. We learnt so much and I could not get enough of God; I had an insatiable hunger for His word and read my Bible at every opportunity.

My husband and I were baptised together; we had a very close relationship and now we were even closer spiritually. I thought I was on cloud nine and that God would bless and bless and answer all my prayers. I thank God I had this grounding.

Four years later, I became ill after a trip to Kariba and a doctor overprescribed Malaquin tablets thinking I might have malaria, which I did not have. I became very ill as a result of this and subsequently had a nervous breakdown. I felt as though I had fallen into a big black hole and couldn't get out; my life was shattered and I wanted to die. I was hospitalised and placed in ward twelve, the psychiatric ward, for four months. Ward twelve was, for me, like hell; it was very frightening and I felt that many people were demonically possessed, which I found very disturbing as I am a very sensitive person. I thought after four long months that I would never be able to get out and I was forced to take medication. I found one of the members of staff to be particularly evil and sadistic and when I spoke of spiritual things they thought I was crazy. On one occasion I experienced a feeling of strangulation and I knew it was evil. I fought back, calling on the name of Jesus, pleading the protection of His precious blood. I did this many times while I was in ward twelve and through these experiences I came to understand the power in Jesus' name. Eventually, in desperation, I managed to run away and get home; but I was not allowed to see my pastor or other Christians, and for a long period I was agitated and restless and experienced difficulty in communicating with people, feeling hopeless often.

Unfortunately, after one year I threw away my tablets too suddenly, without permission from the psychiatrist and a year later had another nervous breakdown. I was hospitalised again and this time underwent shock treatment. Following this I experienced depression as a result of the psychiatrist telling me I was schizophrenic and must have medication for the rest of my life and must accept that fact. I had also gained weight as a result of the medicine and I felt unattractive. My mind was in a state of confusion and I questioned where the Lord was in all of this. My husband became very angry with God and my children could not understand all that was going on.

Fortunately, at this time I did not know that my husband was having an affair with another woman. I discovered at the end of 1979 that he had been having a serious affair with a widow during this period, lasting for five years or more, while I was ill and struggling for my sanity. I felt grieved, rejected and humiliated. The affair started very soon after my first breakdown and he, I am sure, thought I was never going to recover. I fought for our marriage, blaming myself, as I realised that the depression was partly to blame for all that was happening in our lives. I was terrified of being institutionalised again. I was very much against divorce, but a break from each other was necessary. After six months separation we came together again. This was in 1980. Soon after I started to suffer from terrible migraine headaches due to hormonal change and this continued for years. I also had back trouble due to picking up a heavy object. My husband had always been in the habit of drinking, but now his drinking got steadily worse. I still loved him very much and apart from this our marriage was fairly normal and happy. We had many family get-togethers, holidays and boat trips. My daughter also started to drink heavily from about this time; she was then 15 years old, and this caused further strain in our marriage. My husband never gave me enough support to help her and didn't think there was a problem. She and I had many confrontations.

During these 16 years, and since the affair, I had a number of anxiety attacks lasting two or three weeks, particularly in the last five years. During this time the drinking and abuse was very bad and my husband constantly belittled me in public or ignored me. I felt very insecure, afraid and unloved. In 1994 I felt suicidal and my husband told me I was being dramatic when I told him I wanted to die.

I began to suspect that he was having an affair again but he constantly denied it, calling me names, and telling everyone, including the children, how suspicious I was and blaming me for the breakdown in our marriage. Once again I was in torment and became very quick tempered, and retaliated. I felt like Job, asking God "Why?" Why, as a Christian did I have something wrong with my brain, a tormenting, alcoholic husband, and my daughter also an alcoholic, living in sexual sin and ruining her life; my whole family falling away from God, this tormenting illness, schizophrenia or depression, 20 years of sporadic attacks; the stigma of being a mental case and an ineffectual Christian witness? What had I done wrong? So few people understood me, even Christians.

I kept praying and at the end of 1994 I visited Beryl Shaw and received counselling, going way back into my past and praying through all the hurtful areas in my life, especially the fears. It was such a relief to find someone who understood me. The Lord miraculously delivered me from fear (the root of my problems). Initially I was unaware of the extent of the healing that took place on that first visit. When I had arrived at Beryl's, I was numb from the top of my head and down my neck and shoulders. It was not until I arrived home that I realised that the numbness had gone and a great burden had been lifted. When I visited Beryl the second week I was a different person. God is so good! I grew from strength to strength and my family noticed the change in me; even my eyes looked different.

Two years later, in 1996, I discovered in an unbelievable way that my husband was having another serious affair, this time with a close friend. It had been going on for a long time and there were large financial dealings also involved. I was shocked and stunned, my heart ached and I called on the Lord in agony. "I cannot take any more!" I said, and immediately felt a tremendous heat spreading through the whole of my body, starting below my heart. Suddenly I felt incredible strength. Everyone was amazed, including my husband. I was in complete control of the situation, but he was in a state of panic and kept saying, "God is with you! God is with you!" and did not seem to know what to do.

The strength God gave me was supernatural. The Lord sent wonderful friends into my life to help, support and pray for me. The woman my husband was involved with divorced her husband a few months later and they have been living together now for a year. One of the things I had been afraid of was being alone, especially if my husband stopped loving me for someone else. I thought it would destroy me totally, but this is a lie of the devil. God says he will never leave us or forsake us, and *it is true*. I have very seldom been lonely. Even when I am alone I am at peace and enjoy the silence. The Bible says, "Your Maker is your husband" (Isaiah 54: 5). Praise the Lord.

My fight for sanity has been like going to hell and back, and if I had not been a committed Christian I would not have come through. Now I feel free and have not had another attack since Beryl prayed for me, even with the long and continuous divorce proceedings still going on. I realise that my husband's continual drinking, abuse and womanising, involving long serious affairs (and others), were very much to blame for the anxiety attacks I had over the last 16 year period. My medication has been cut down already by the doctor and when this is all over I hope to come off it completely. Everyone is amazed. I am joyful and happy. So many people have commented on the change they see in me and I am enjoying the Christian fellowship I had been craving. I refuse to allow my husband's affairs to destroy me.

My life is very different now; I found the social scene so empty and hectic. I'm all out for Jesus now and very involved with the church, other people and hobbies. I have always enjoyed cooking, sewing, flower arranging, gardening and painting, but I especially love the people God has sent into my life and my family and I marvel at how unique we all are. I feel that I am on the threshold of something very big in my life.

Already the Lord is using my home to minister to others experiencing similar circumstances to mine, which is confirmation of a prophecy previously received. Monthly meetings are being held for single, divorced and hurting people and the Lord is blessing the gatherings. I had been afraid of being incapable of supporting myself due to my lack of qualifications and the fact that I am not an intellectual person. However, the Lord has shown me how He can use the gifts that He has blessed me with and I am reminded of His word which states, "But seek first His kingdom and His righteousness; and all these things shall be added to you" (Matthew 6: 33).

My divorce is taking a long time but coming through with amazing miracles and God is revealing hidden truths; He is working with the lawyers in my favour, protecting me, and is restoring me with finances I knew nothing about. How true is God's word which states, *"No weapon formed against us will stand"* (Isaiah 54: 17).

I have experienced tremendous grief and pain over the loss of our marriage. Many years of sharing with one partner is a lot to lose and I have given the best years of my life, but the Lord has promised me that my last years will be the best and they are still to come. He is restoring the years the locusts have eaten (Joel 2: 25) and I will reclaim everything the evil one has taken from me, and more. I am looking forward to my future, with or without a husband. I do not feel afraid of the future and I believe many more wonderful miracles are on their way with my loved ones and family. I believe they will come back to God and I keep praying for my husband and the other woman, especially for their precious souls. I believe he will present the Gospel one day.

Thank God I held on, sometimes by a thread; sometimes not even praying, just reading the Bible, not giving up; sometimes even compromising. I realise now that through all this time the Lord has been carrying me and I was upheld and sustained by the prayers of fellow Christians, particularly one special friend who gave me so much love and support over many years and still continues to pray for me.

Looking back I see that God taught me so much during those 20 years of hell and through all the struggling and suffering in my mind, without me realising it, I have grown tremendously in faith and in knowledge of the word of God. I now have a deeper understanding of the power in the Word of God and the application of it in my life. I have learned not to worry, but to hand things over to God and pray and trust. I am weak but strong in the Lord and I know that without Him I could never have come through. God causes everything to work together for good to those who love Him and are called according to His purpose (Romans 8: 28). This is true and I know that God has a purpose and plan in all of it. I am expecting great things, like Job when he was restored.

One of my mistakes, I know now, was to depend too much on my husband; we can only depend on the Lord, not man. I should have dealt with my fears a long time ago, but God was also teaching me patience. I was very impatient and still battle with that. I still have a long way to go spiritually and on occasions when I think back to the early years of my marriage to my closest and dearest, and the love we shared, and compare him with the stranger of today it causes me great sadness, but the Lord's timing is always perfect. I find forgiveness is the key to answered prayer. This is not always easy but it means to forgive, forgive and forgive.

The scriptures I held on to time and time again are: *"We shall not grow weary in well-doing, for in due season we shall reap if we do not lose heart"* (Galatians 6: 9); and, *"We do not have a spirit of fear, but one of love, power and a sound mind"* (2 Timothy 1: 7). I have overcome through the precious word of Jesus and His victory on Calvary.

"Victory Over Evil"
Anonymous

I was born in December 1939 in Belfast, Northern Ireland, and was told by my mother that I was a wee mistake as I came along eight years after my brother and sister. When my mother went into labour dad went to call the doctor, and my godmother, who lived next door. By the time the doctor arrived I was lying there on the bed. He said, "What a lovely bundle of joy you have there for Christmas." I was named Agnes Evelyn after two aunts, but was always called Joy.

I was brought up Baptist, and at four years old started attending the Antrim Road Baptist Primary School. My Aunt Agnes belonged to the Salvation Army, and when she visited my mum on Wednesday evenings I had to stand on a stool and tell her what Bible stories I had learned.

My brother had a good job with a construction company in Belfast and earned good money, so he spoiled me and Mum. He even bought me a Lambretta scooter, which was all the rage in Ireland at that time. My girlfriend also had a scooter, and so four of us girls, two Catholics and two Protestants used to go out touring and to Youth Hostels. In those days it was difficult, for Catholics and Protestants did not mix, and I was told especially not to go out with Catholic boys. When I asked why not, my mother told me that if I married a Catholic I would have to agree to bring up my children as Catholics, and that would be against our religion.

I came out to Zimbabwe (then Rhodesia) when I was 21 and was married soon after. Our first son was only a year old when I received my first major hurt, for up till then very little had bothered me. I received a telegram saying that my mother was dying. I managed to get on the first plane out, but when I arrived in Belfast my brother told me I was too late. My mother had died while I was travelling. I was deeply shocked and distressed at not having been able to talk to her and say "Good-bye" and I blamed God for many years.

Although I knew what I had been taught, and had even attended Billy Graham Crusades, I had never accepted Jesus as my Saviour and Lord and now I rebelled completely, turning away from the church and God.

My husband and I had three sons, and had them all dedicated at Elgin Road Baptist Church. They all had to go to Sunday school, but I was still doing my own thing. We attended any plays or concerts the boys were in, and our lives continued on smoothly.

Then when I was about 36, a missionary from Penhalonga (who had actually given me away at my wedding) came to visit. He had known my mother well and we spoke a lot about her. As a result of these talks I saw where I had been wrong, and knowing about the Resurrection, I realized that I would never see my mother again unless I repented my past behaviour and got my priorities in the correct order. I truly accepted Christ that day and it was wonderful.

A while later, due to various difficulties, we decided to return to Ireland, but I could not settle back there, so after a year we sold everything and returned here, landing with nothing. We managed to rent a fully furnished flat, and a year later we bought another home

Our oldest son moved to South Africa, and married a South African girl. Sadly, the marriage broke down due to the situation in that country; and she left my son and divorced him. I felt sick in the situation as there had never before been a divorce in either of our families. In fact, divorce is a word never even spoken in Ireland. Our son returned home three years ago. Before the divorce he had undergone a major stomach operation. When we arrived at his home in South Africa for a visit I just stared in amazement at what I saw; a young man standing looking as if he were dying of AIDS. He had lost about 20 kilogrammes. Before getting out of the car I asked God to give me the strength not to show my hurt and amazement, which He did. On the way home I lost control of myself and started to cry and shout at my husband that our son was dying.

As a result of believing that he was dying I had a nervous breakdown, and then went into a state of chronic depression. I have had my uterus removed and twice had lumps removed, but never had I felt like this. I was unable to walk, or even get out of bed; I totally withdrew from everything and everyone. I understood why some people commit suicide.

I visited many doctors, who knew what the problem was and called it endogenous depression, or a depression that originates from inside one's self. I was unable to reach out to God, and He seemed far away. I was told by many people to "Pull yourself together! It's all in your mind." Yes, they were correct, it was all in my mind, but what they did not understand was that it was as much a sickness as a broken leg.

During a "good" week we travelled to South Africa for a short holiday, but we were involved in a car accident. My husband suffered broken ribs, and I had 36 stitches above my left eye. I returned worse than I was before and went back into my bed for weeks.

I met a friend one day who told me she had experienced the same thing that I had and recommended a psychiatrist. I had four visits but there was no improvement. I felt utterly helpless and defeated. I was no good for anything. There were good days and bad days, which came without warning. During the good days I was able to stop blaming and questioning God. My missionary friend gave me a book called, *Your Healing is Within You,* (Canon Jim Glennon, Published by Bridge Logos Pub. 1980); it's a wonderful book which I read and reread. Although I believed all Jesus' promises in the New Testament, I still could not rise above my depression, and knew that only the Almighty could help me.

One day a lady who did not know my situation spoke of Beryl Shaw, and during our conversation mentioned that Beryl was involved in the Inner Healing ministry. The Lord impressed on my heart that I had to phone Beryl, which I did, and we made our first appointment. That was in September 1994.

On the day of our appointment I had great difficulty with driving the car. Since our accident I had not driven much, and some days I was not even able to get through our gates and on to the road. I would sometimes get out on to the road and suddenly experience panic attacks. I would start off for town, and after a few hundred metres along the road my hands and body would start to sweat, I would begin shaking and then feel faint so I was lying over the steering wheel. After what seemed like hours I would get back some strength, reverse, and drive back home as quickly as possible. It got so bad I was eventually housebound, and had to walk everywhere. It was impossible for me to drive in town. That morning I started to shake, my legs went weak, and I had palpitations of the heart. I knew that Satan was trying to prevent my healing, and I was able to stand firm in the Lord, and went to my meeting

My healing started that day and continued visit by visit. It was not an instantaneous, or overnight healing, but a gradual one. For five years I had been ill, but the last year has seen the mighty working of God in my life and my illness. I was even able to drive to town and back by myself, which I had not been able to do for three years since the accident. On my return I had to phone Beryl and tell her what I had done. I give God all the glory for using Beryl in my healing in spirit, body and mind.

Some months later I did experience one serious satanic attack. I had dropped a friend at Beryl's house for prayer, and was due to collect her later. I do not know what came over me but Satan started attacking my mind with negative thoughts – "Oh! You think you have been delivered from your sickness do you? What a joke! Do you believe that? Let's see you get into that car to pick up your friend." At first I froze completely, and then I gathered enough strength to phone Beryl. In tears I said to her, "Beryl, I cannot come! I cannot get into the car." Well, Beryl prayed for me over the phone, and commanded Satan to leave me alone. She said that I did not belong to him, and he was a defeated foe, and I was covered in the precious blood of Jesus. Beryl insisted that I stand firm against the devil and get into the car, and that she and my friend would cover me with prayer as I drove to her house. I went out running, and drove again like a bird, and of course I knew Beryl and my friend were deep in prayer for me until my arrival. I did have a few tears, but, praise God, it has never happened again.

I now do not hesitate to say that as a result of the healing that has gone on in my body, spirit, and particularly my mind, even though I have been severely attacked with hurtful words, the miracle is that I no longer just lie on my bed with chronic depression, and unable to walk. My mind is on God's word and His promises, and uppermost in my mind is the knowledge that Satan has been defeated.

A song that we sing at church which is very meaningful to me has the words, "Give thanks, with a grateful heart, give thanks unto the Holy One; give thanks because He's given Jesus Christ, His Son. . . and now let the weak say 'I am strong', and let the poor say 'I am rich' because of what the Lord has done. . . for me. . . give thanks." (GIVE THANKS WAS WRITTEN

BY PRESTON, BILLY / JONES, DOUGLAS EARL AND WAS PUBLISHED BY LYRICS © UNIVERSAL MUSIC PUBLISHING GROUP, MEMORY LANE MUSIC GROUP, EMI MUSIC PUBLISHING)

I just cry, and the Holy Spirit fills my heart with the joy of what He has done; they are not tears of sorrow. No, instead they are tears of love, joy and thanks.

It has been a new beginning for me, and the Lord has brought other ladies in to my life. These people have experienced the same as I did, so I can talk to them of my healing, and encourage them.

I am still often hurt by things that people may say or do, but I can now rise above the hurts and show love to them. There is still a lot of healing, and changes to be made in my life, but, as I have said, I no longer lie on my bed depressed, as I know the power of God in my life.

I end with a verse that to me is very lovely:

"I know who holds the future and guides me with His hand;
With God, things just don't happen, everything is planned.
So as I face tomorrow with its problems great and small,
I will trust the God of miracles, and give to Him my all."

(LYRIC FROM THE CHORUS OF "I DO NOT KNOW WHAT LIES AHEAD" WRITTEN BY ALFRED B. SMITH AND EUGENE CLARKE. PUBLISHED BY NEW SPRING © COPYRIGHT 1958. ADMINISTERED. BY UNIVERSAL MUSIC PUBLISHING MGB AUSTRALIA PTY LIMITED)

CHAPTER SIXTEEN

Sorrow and Triumph

"There is neither Jew nor Greek, there is neither slave nor free man, there is neither male nor female; for you are all one in Christ Jesus." Galatians 3: 28.

It was good to know that the Lord was with us in all circumstances, whether good or bad. Through the "highs" and the "lows" He never failed us. The following story is one of sadness and of triumph in the face of adversity.

One very special member of the Hatfield Presbyterian Church, to which we belonged, was Angeline Matare. Angeline was a beautiful dynamic Christian, who loved and served the Lord. She was a black African and belonged to the Shona tribe in Zimbabwe. When I first met Angeline at a Bible Study I was immediately attracted by her lovely smile. She was expecting her third child. We soon got to know Angeline well and were interested in the progress of her pregnancy. Eventually little Felicity was born – a beautiful baby. Everyone loved her and took turns in carrying her around. Our minister's wife was very especially attached to her, and frequently looked after her. However, as the months went by we noticed that Felicity was constantly sick, and did not appear to be making the same progress as other children of her age. We were all concerned, and prayers were constantly prayed for her and the family. Eventually, to the shock of all, little Felicity was diagnosed as suffering from AIDS. It was difficult to accept that this beautiful little girl would probably never even reach the age of five years old. Angeline was very unwell for many months, and our minister's wife and another member of the congregation looked after Felicity faithfully, for months on end. When she was just under four years old little Felicity died. The funeral service was conducted at the church, where many people gathered to support the family and convey their condolences. To see Angeline so distraught was heart rending, but, as always, her faith triumphed, and she requested that Sue and I sing a favourite song of hers at the service, "Have Faith in God."

Some months later Angeline was asked if she would be prepared to be interviewed concerning the loss of her daughter to AIDS, from which she was also suffering. Angeline was very nervous and apprehensive, but agreed; we upheld her with our prayers. After this, she was asked to speak on radio, and then in schools, also on the same subject. Within the space of one or two years she was travelling around the country sharing her testimony with thousands of people, and eventually she was asked to attend AIDS conferences in Britain, France and in the United States. Who would ever have thought that our gentle Angeline would be used by the Lord in such an important field? To Him be all the glory for strengthening and equipping her to fulfil such a difficult task. I would now like to share a testimony written by Angeline during her time of sickness that I have previously referred to.

The Wonderful Vision of Healing
Angeline Matare

Our Lord can heal.

In July 1987 I experienced the healing of the Lord. I was in hospital lying on my pillows, and as I faced the door it would not have been possible for anyone to enter or leave the room without me seeing them.

There was no doubt that I was on the death row. I was on my way to death. After one and a half months in hospital, and being told that there was no cure for me, I felt life was hopeless. The last thing I did was to put myself under God's protection. "Not my will, but Thine, be done."

During the night I started coughing up thick phlegm and I was finding it very difficult to breathe. I could feel the tiredness of death was upon me. I cried in my mother's language, 'Mwari wangu. Mwari wangu, mandisireiko pane ino nguva?' meaning, 'My Lord. My Lord, why do you forsake me at this hour?' I repeated the same words several times. Then suddenly, I heard beside my bed, to the right, a voice which said, "Woman, you see the way you are coughing and passing out this phlegm; that is going to be the end of your disease." I did not like to answer without seeing who was speaking. Although I was unable to walk, or turn in the bed by myself, I could generally turn my head from side to side, but I was unable to at that moment. When the voice spoke a second time I tried again to turn my head. I managed to turn it a little, and then saw a white garment; it was as white as snow. I cried, repeating the same words again. The voice spoke again, repeating the same message a third time. I decided to answer, and asked, 'Are you sure?' The voice said, 'Yes,' and spoke in my mother's language. I stayed like that, seeing the long white garment until it was dawn, and that is when I managed to turn my head toward the voice. There was nobody there. The owner of the voice had disappeared.

From that moment I believed that I was healed, because nobody could have left the room without me seeing them. "Believing is Healing."

Early in the morning the doctor came, and said, "Now we know what we can do for you. We will call the physiotherapist to give you some exercises that will cough out the fluid in your lungs. Your lungs are full of fluid. If you cough out this fluid you will feel fine."

After three months of hospitalisation, and three months of physiotherapy I was discharged feeling much better, and went home weighing 42 kilogrammes instead of 55. At present my weight is between 57 and 60 kilogrammes. He is a God of miracles and wonders.

To tell the truth, I was brought up by a Christian grandmother and I grew up as a Christian, but my faith wasn't as strong as it is now. I used to think that worshipping God was for the whites only, for I had never seen a picture of Jesus in black imagination. But now I believe there is only one living God that is three in one.

From the day I was saved and the Lord, our God, restored my life I am now living by faith in His Son, the Lord Jesus Christ, who died for me on the cross, and it's no longer I who live, but Christ that lives in me.

CHAPTER SEVENTEEN

Unswerving Devotion

"But you shall receive power when the Holy Spirit has come upon you; and you shall be My witnesses both in Jerusalem, and in all Judea and Samaria, and even to the remotest part of the earth." Acts 1: 8.

It was a privilege to get to know many of the Shona people in the church congregation. I admired their simple, but very strong faith in God. In the early 1990's, Talkmore Chilanga, later to be Rev. Chilanga, was a member of the church and I would like to share the following testimony, which he wrote. This testimony is a tribute to his strong faith, and implicit trust in God's provision for his life.

Testimony of Talkmore Chilanga

Imagine this: You come from a well-to-do family. All your brothers and sisters are well-educated, and they are earning more than they need. They are trying to make your life as good as theirs. They have sent you to an expensive, multi-racial primary school, and you are the only one in the area in which you live who attends such a school. However, these close relatives of yours are not Christians, and you are. You later discover that all the favours they are doing for you are conditional – they want you to join them in their religion. To make matters worse, they forbid you to do any form of Christian work. You are forced to join them and participate in their religion.

This is what I faced in my Christian life.

I was born in 1969 at Nyanga General Hospital, where my father was working as a nurse. In 1972 my father was transferred from Nyanga General Hospital to the Eastern Highlands Tea Estates Clinic. In 1975 war broke out in the Eastern Highlands of Zimbabwe. My parents decided to join the liberation war, together with other citizens of Zimbabwe.

My brothers and sisters were sent to stay in Kwekwe with my uncle, who is the principal of the Islamic Propagation Centre. As I was a sickly child, my parents decided to take me with them to Mozambique. Once in Mozambique, my parents were sent to Tanzania for training, and I stayed with my uncle who was working for the Zambian Embassy.

In 1976 I started schooling at a Roman Catholic Church School. I lived a life of luxury, and will probably never have such luxury again during the rest of my life on earth. I received an education from Grade One to Grade Seven.

During this time I became friends with a Catholic priest, and it was during this time that God began to work in my life. Although some Protestants are opposed to the Catholics, I must give them the credit for bringing Jesus into my life. It is probable that without them I would not have become a Christian.

After the war I remained in Mozambique until December 1982, when I returned to Zimbabwe. I was happy to be reunited with my family again.

In 1983 I started Grade two at Macheke Primary School, which is a boarding school near Marondera. I was there from Grade Two to Grade Four, and during these three years came in contact with Mr. Gustastof, who was a member of Emergence Mission. It was through this man that I was baptised. I was selected to lead a prayer group, and as I was the oldest pupil at the school I was appointed president of the Christian Disciplinary Committee.

In 1986, when I was about to start Grade Five, I was told by my brothers to leave school because they wanted me to go to Waterfalls in Harare to join in studying the Quran at the Islamic Propagation Centre. I tried to refuse, but was unsuccessful. Since I was still a minor I had to go whether I liked it or not, and there was no way I could have stood up for my rights.

I studied the Quran for two years, 1986, and 1987. In 1987, when I went home for the December holidays, I told my brothers that I did not want to study the Quran any more, and that I wanted to return to school. They just laughed when they heard an 18-year-old boy say that he wanted to go back to do primary schooling.

The following year, 1988, I started Grade Seven. It was hard, and I had to struggle to achieve my objectives. During the same year my father suffered from a stroke and was paralysed, and was sent to South Africa for an operation. At the same time my brothers ordered me to leave home because I was involved in Christian activities, which they had forbidden. I had to leave school, and home, and did not know where to go. I just packed my suitcase and left.

I moved from house to house, asking the richer people for a job, but none of them could help me. Those who were kind gave me a meal, and others gave me some place to sleep. I lived in this manner for a month, and at times had to sell my clothes to get money for food.

At the end of December 1988, God opened a wide door for me. I went to Honde Valley Mission looking for any kind of work from the teachers who were there. After receiving negative answers from one teacher after another I finally decided to leave, but then saw that there was one house that I had not called at.

I went to the house and knocked. A white man came to the door and looked at me with a very fierce expression. Seeing this, I lost all hope. "What do you want?" he asked me in a thick voice. I told him that I was looking for any type of work. He invited me into his home and motioned me to sit on a chair beside a table. I sat down, and he brought me a mug full of cold drink, and some biscuits. I remembered what my mother used to tell me: "Do not judge the depth of a pool by looking at its surface."

After I had finished the drink that he had given me, and the biscuits, he took my empty plate and mug and washed them. He then came to sit at the table, and began to ask questions. I told him my life story.

He asked me if I still wanted to go back to school, and I told him that I did want to. He gave me a job, working in his house, cooking, doing laundry and cleaning the floors. I worked for him for two weeks, and then he told me that he wanted me to accompany him to Kariba. We stayed there for eight days, and during this time he told me that he had decided that I should attend the school where he was teaching – Honde Valley Mission. I nearly cried when I heard this news from a stranger that I had only known for two weeks. I began to see how God works in a person's life. I recalled what God says in the Bible, "I will go before you and make the crooked places straight! I will cut in pieces the gates of brass....I will give thee the treasures of darkness and the hidden riches of secret places! (Isaiah 45: 2 – 3a) So it was that at the age of 20, in 1989, I started Form One.

When my brothers heard that I was going to school, they went to the court and accused the man of adopting me illegally. Fortunately they lost the case. I stayed at Honde Valley Mission School from Form One to Form Four, and when I finished Form Four in 1992, I was employed at Arda Katiyo Tea Estates as a dispatch clerk.

In April 1993, I got a place to be trained as a nurse at Parirenyatwa Hospital in Harare, starting in September 1994, but in September 1993, I got a vacancy at Harare Theological College, to train as a theologian. Thank God for the way that He is keeping me through other people.

Talkmore Chilanga.

....

I remember an occasion when Talkmore asked me to pray for protection for him. He was planning to visit his family in the Eastern Highlands and was not expecting a friendly welcome. We were concerned for him and covered him in prayer for the duration of his visit. On his return he told us that he was not even allowed to go into his home, but that his brothers chased him away with axes. They were not even prepared to speak to him.

In spite of the persecution aimed at him by his family, this brave man remained strong in his faith and his commitment to the Lord. He remained a member of the Hatfield Church and completed his theological training. Eventually Talkmore received a call as minister to another congregation and some months later Mervyn and I were privileged to attend the induction service. It was also a joy to meet his new wife and to learn that he was greatly loved and accepted by his congregation.

It is wonderful to know that when God has a calling upon a person's life, there is nothing that can thwart His plan. He opens and closes doors at His will and according to His perfect timing. I now share another example of the outworking of God's mighty plan in the life of another Shona member of the congregation. Rev. Wilbert Sayimani Musara, like Talkmore, had worshipped with us for some years, during which time he attended a Bible College and trained for the ministry. It was a pleasure to work with Wilbert, he was always smiling, respectful and cooperative. The more I learnt of his life, the more I admired the courage that he displayed in his walk with the Lord.

The following is a testimony written by Wilbert in 1997.

God Can Change Lives

I feel very grateful to live and tell what the Lord has done for me. It is so great that I cannot help but tell it to people each time I get a chance. For this reason, I am quite happy writing part of it down as another way of shouting it out.

I never thought my life would be what it is now. I remember in 1977 talking to my granny with tears running down my cheeks, in unbearable pain, looking at my life on the verge of destruction. There was my father in front of us lying motionless on his deathbed. In blinding tears and with choking sobs I said to my granny, "This is the end of me going to school: who else is going to pay for my fees?" However, the question was rhetorical. In bewilderment my granny responded in tears as well. She knew for certain that this was a terminal sickness. My father had reached the end of his life span, and eventually he died. At this time I was still in Grade 5.

My brethren, what followed after this is a mystery, and will remain a mystery to me. I hardly believed that I at one point sat for an examination at a university. I still hope to write many more examinations. I know it sounds like a dream, especially to those who knew me after my father died. Frankly, I do not have an adequate explanation as to how my schooling was funded then and now. Brethren, God is real to me.

Because of my situation, having lost my father, having an unemployed mother, and being one of a family of six, (which was later extended as relatives from the communal lands fled the torments of war,) life became very unbearable. The result of this congestion at our home resulted in us becoming a model of poverty in our community.

The consequence of my humbled social status was that I felt unrecognised and unaccepted in society. I knew I could not fit into either the middle or upper levels of society, and so an inferiority complex developed in me. I lived every day beside people who would not look at me as a fellow human being, as the Lord would have them see me. Instead, they would see me and others in the same situation, as trees moving, and not as human beings. Though some of them professed to be

Christians, I always felt that they needed a second touch from Jesus, like the blind man in Mark 8: 24, 25.

My humbled feelings were made even worse when I was first exposed to people of different races and different socio-economic backgrounds. It made me shrink even more, thinking that no-one would ever listen to me or treat me as an equal. Definitely, I felt wounded and bleeding. I had lost my identity in this world. Only Jesus remained to care for and heal me. I had no choice but to take a step of faith, with no reservations, and put all my trust in Jesus, and He helped me in the fullness of time.

I cannot, even now, explain what happened when the flames of His love reached me. Looking at the example and ministry of Jesus Christ, with His light shining on me, for the first time I started to feel self-acceptance. God started pointing out my abilities and potential, thus challenging me to take a step out of my depressed situation, where there was not even an iota of self-esteem, and therefore void of any self-acceptance. Today I unhesitatingly stand to say that God liberated me from mental bondage and stagnation, where the devil was causing me not to work for God because I felt I was a nobody, and was thus assisting those who mocked me. I am glad now I know that I am just like anyone created in the image of God.

Look what God did in the end: It is very surprising that if I speak now, people listen. If there is a task for me in the house of the Lord, I no longer fear being watched by different people. I simply do what I am supposed to do. Truthfully, brethren, there has not been a physical change in me. I am still the same person, only now I am someone who has experienced the redemptive and liberating power of Jesus Christ. I am now free in Christ Jesus. Oh, how I love such a God who freed and changed my life. Indeed, God is a good God. I will forever learn from Jesus Christ how He identified with the poor, the oppressed and the marginalised, so making His message relevant to their situation, with the object of setting them free and bringing a sense of self worth. No wonder Jesus said, "The Spirit of the Lord is upon Me, because He anointed Me to preach the gospel to the poor. He has sent Me to proclaim release to the captives, and recovery of sight to the blind, to set free those who are downtrodden, to proclaim the favourable day of the Lord." (Luke 4: 18,19)

This is my testimony, brethren; I was downtrodden and now am set free. I was poor and now am rich in Jesus Christ, and the good news was also preached to me. I am no longer a captive. I was unlearned, and am now learned in Christ Jesus. My final words to crown it all are, "Brethren, I will never ever leave the cross of Jesus, from where I got my deliverance. He is the author and finisher of my life. I will worship Him until He comes again.

Wilbert Sayimani Musara.

....

The Lord continued to bless and provide for Wilbert and his family. He became the minister of a local church and in the years that followed he furthered his theological training in South Africa.

CHAPTER EIGHTEEN

Power to Witness

"And it will come about after this that I will pour out My Spirit on all mankind; And your sons and daughters will prophesy, your old men will dream dreams, your young men will see visions. And even on the male and female servants I will pour out My Spirit in those days." Joel 2: 28, 29.

Angeline, Talkmore and Wilbert were only three of the many African Christian believers in Zimbabwe. It was not easy for African Christians to stand against the tribal beliefs of their families and they faced dangers of many kinds. However, in spite of much opposition, they remained strong in their faith and God blessed them with courage and strength. In the midst of difficulties and the ongoing changes taking place in the country, God was causing a mighty outpouring of His Holy Spirit to fall upon people of all races.

An organisation that I greatly admired had the name of Operation Foxfire. (The name was based on the story of Sampson when he sent the foxes in amongst the Philistine crops to destroy them, Judges 15.) Christians underwent training in evangelism and then were sent out in pairs to evangelise amongst the people in the rural areas. They lived and worked alongside the people in the villages, undertaking any tasks given them, sometimes spending many weeks in one village. Through their efforts hundreds of people were saved and brought into the Kingdom of God. It was exciting and encouraging to read the testimonies of what God was doing in the lives of people, and to learn of the miracles that He was performing.

Because of the African belief in ancestral worship, and their understanding of the reality and power of evil, it was easy to converse with them about God and the existence of the Holy Spirit. Also, it was easy to talk about the reality of demonic forces. Consequently the Foxfire teams enjoyed tremendous success and were greatly blessed in their efforts.

Because of the environment that we lived in, at one stage we, (the leadership, at Hatfield,) were concerned about the spiritual welfare of the church and the lack of growth in numbers. We decided to spend time praying in and around the buildings and the grounds. In previous years the ground on which the church had been built had been vacant, and could have been used for any purpose. Amongst African people the practice of witchcraft was common, and it would not have surprised us to know that ceremonies had been performed on the land. Had this been the case it would have had an adverse effect upon Christian worship taking place on the same land. It was therefore necessary for us to establish the truth of what *had* taken place. At one point four of us were standing, praying beneath a large tree in the courtyard when I had a rather unpleasant vision. Very clearly I saw several people squatting around a fire, which was built on the ground. Hanging above the fire was a large black pot and floating around in the water in the pot were several eyes. The eyes meant nothing to me, but the vision did establish the fact that ceremonies had taken place on the land. As a result we prayed further as the Lord led us and also decided to carry out further cleansing of the land at a second meeting.

The following day I was in conversation with one of those who had been involved in the prayers and spoke to him about the eyes in the pot. This man was a member of the police force and had intimate knowledge of African practices. He explained to me that some of the rituals and sacrifices involved the use of body parts, in the belief that they would bring healing or enhance human senses. The eyes could have been used in the belief that they would bring deeper insight or vision. It amazed me to think that at the time of the prayer meeting, our friend had been aware of these facts, whereas I had been totally ignorant. So often, throughout the years, the visions that I received appeared nonsensical, or even bizarre, but I learnt the importance of speaking out and sharing what I saw before me. God always had His good reasons and different ways of imparting knowledge, and we had to be obedient to His guidance no matter how strange or meaningless it might have appeared to us.

Something that I have always found exciting is the variety of ways in which God ministers to us. The Holy Spirit cannot be boxed in and He rarely reveals Himself in the same way twice. Therefore, His ministrations take us by surprise and leave us standing in awe of His power and might.

I remember a time when I went with a group to listen to a visiting speaker at a friend's church. The evening started with a time of praise and was followed by a powerful message. During the time of ministry at the end of the programme I was led to go forward to receive prayer. The Holy Spirit was moving in a most powerful way and several people around me had fallen under the power. There had been times when I was sceptical about the way people had fallen down at meetings, and questioned whether the phenomenon was really of God or not. As I stood at the front of the church with my eyes closed I remember saying to the Lord, "I am *not* just going to fall down, if I go down I *have* to know that it's of You." With that I received a tremendous blow on the side of my leg, which buckled my knees and down I went! Very softly! I couldn't believe what had happened. There had been no one close to me so I hadn't been knocked down by some other person, and the blow had not been painful. I have a clear memory of lying on the floor for some while, during which time I experienced the most wonderful peace of God. At a later stage my prayer request was granted.

Following our time of prayer in which God had confirmed our belief that sacrifices had been carried out on the Hatfield Church grounds, a second date was set for further prayer. It was decided that the minister, Sue and I would anoint the church, and all outside buildings, including the hall, and claim the buildings back for the Lord. We spent a great deal of time working our way through the premises, anointing various items and spending time in prayer. Eventually we finished in the grounds between the outside wall of the office block and the boundary fence. I remember saying to Sue and the minister, "Shall we end off in prayer here or go inside?" It was agreed that we would close off in prayer where we stood. The three of us stood side by side. We each held a cup containing the remainder of the oil, which we had been using. As we closed our eyes in prayer I was immediately given a vision, it was the same vision that I had been given at a prayer meeting in the church the day before. The scene before me was one of awesome beauty. Myriads of angels in shining white hovered above the roof of the church; in their midst, in radiant glory, was the Lord of Hosts. His arm was held high and in His hand He held a huge sword. As soon as I saw this amazing scene before me I simply said, "Oh Lord," and briefly described what was before me. No sooner had the words left my lips when I fell straight down flat on my face! Anyone who knows Africa will know that the ground is rock hard. I landed on my face right between two huge rocks about a metre in height. (Trying to describe it afterwards, I likened the sensation of hitting the hard, dusty ground, to that of a solid, wooden door falling down flat, accompanied by a dull, "whoof" sound.) I did not feel a thing, but I was acutely aware of oil running all over my head and face! As I lay there in the dust I remember thinking, "Oh dear, I've just washed and set my hair and I'm wearing my new blue top!" I was also *very* aware of the Lord's presence and it was wonderful to be enveloped in His warmth and love. As I lay there I gathered that the minister must have made a move to pick me up, because I faintly recall Sue saying, "No, leave her." She was well aware of what had taken place. Eventually I did get up, feeling somewhat sheepish because I was covered in oil and dust and looked an absolute sight! Sue explained to me afterwards that as I fell down, my hand had knocked the cup she was holding in her hand. It was the oil in her cup that had run all over me.

This experience, like others, once again left us standing in awe of our Almighty God. It was very difficult to believe that I had fallen face down on rock hard ground and had not felt a thing. Neither did I suffer any bruising whatsoever. Also the fact that I had fallen between two huge rocks, even a glancing blow on the side of one could have seriously grazed my face. But I was totally unscathed and even my new, blue top washed out well and left not a trace of oil!

CHAPTER NINETEEN

Radical Discipleship

"For those who are according to the flesh set their minds on the things of the flesh, but those who are according to the Spirit, the things of the Spirit. For the mind set on the flesh is death, but the mind set on the Spirit is life and peace."
Romans 8: 5, 6

Over the years the Lord had impressed upon us the need to cleanse our homes and keep them in a way that would be glorifying to Him. We needed to pay attention to the items that we allowed to come into our homes, and also to those things we kept. Beautiful gifts, of varying kinds, had been given to us by innocent, well-meaning friends and relatives, and some items had come from other countries. Unfortunately some, although attractive, were not acceptable in a Christian home and could be used against us to thwart our spiritual growth.

Often, when ornaments are fashioned at the hands of people who worship other gods, prayers are prayed over the objects. These can become known as " familiar objects." Sometimes a curse can be placed upon an item. Whether it is a familiar object or a curse, it can be carried on the object to any destination. When brought into a home, there is a distinct possibility of whatever the object is carrying, affecting the well-being of those living there.

When God opened the way for the Israelites to enter the promised land, He not only told them to destroy the idolatrous nations before them, (Deuteronomy 7: 1, 2) neither to intermarry with them, (verses 3,4,) but also to "tear down their altars, and smash their *sacred* pillars, and hew down their Asherim, and burn their graven images with fire." (Verse 5) The people were not only warned to carry out these instructions, but also commanded not to bring abominations into their houses. (verses 25, 26.) Only then would they be free to enjoy the promises of God. (verses 12 – 15.) They were to be set apart as God's chosen people. (Read also ACTS 19: 18, 19.)

As Mervyn and I had some knowledge in this area, some of our friends asked us to come into their homes and give our opinion on certain objects. They also requested that we pray through their homes, consecrating the building to the Lord. One such request came from a dear friend who had recently lost her husband. "Tiger," (her nickname retained from her childhood,) contacted us and requested that we visit her home and examine the ornaments. She was adamant that her home should be cleansed of any item that may not be glorifying to the Lord. I phoned another friend, Terry*, who had a great deal of experience in this area, requesting that he accompanied Mervyn and me to Tiger's home, some 20 miles from the city. Tiger's late husband had been a collector of African artefacts and on their travels throughout Africa had constantly added to the collection. We set a date and travelled to the home together. On entering we were amazed to see a wide variety of carved objects of every shape and size. The items were displayed in cabinets that lined the walls of the lounge from the floor almost to the ceiling. Many of the statues and ornaments had been painstakingly and intricately carved. As we viewed the items it was hard to imagine ourselves breaking up the collection and destroying those that we felt led to dispose of. However, Tiger assured us that she wanted the job done and encouraged us to be as ruthless as was necessary. I was so pleased that Terry had accompanied us and we looked to him for clear guidance. Eventually, having removed all that we felt was necessary, the items were placed in a large cardboard box, which we carried out into the garden. We then tipped the contents of the box into a large, clean, metal drum and promptly set fire to it. I do praise the Lord that the home stood alone on spacious grounds in open country, because the thick, black smoke that billowed up from the drum had to be seen to be believed! We all agreed that considering the objects had only been made of wood, they should never have produced the horrendous display of dense blackness that billowed up before us. Following action like this we cannot actually see with our human sight what God has done in the spiritual realm. However, we can testify to some of the positive feed-back we received. People sometimes spoke of "Having been set free in one area or another in their lives." Or "Having experienced a break-through in their spiritual walk with the Lord." In many cases people testified to "A new sense of God's peace and presence in their homes." I think all were in agreement to the fact that their homes felt "cleansed."

In Tiger's case she simply went from strength to strength in her spiritual walk with the Lord. I cannot share details of her life, but I will go so far as to say that living on her own, and travelling long distances in dangerous country every day required tremendous courage. Tiger's implicit trust in the Lord's protection and provision for her life was a tremendous testimony to God's saving grace and power.

I now share the following testimony which was written by Tiger in July 1999 following her conversion.

No More Death or Mourning, or Crying or Pain

I come from a traditional Anglican background – baptised, confirmed, and married in church. I got on with my life, aware that my teaching ability was a gift, but very much in control. I was a 'bossy-boots' teacher who dealt with a home, children, teaching, and helping in the family business and whatever else came along. I knew God was there, but I didn't go to church.

My sister had brain cancer as a child of three. About 12 years ago, aged 34, she took 18 months to die a truly awful death. I blamed God – not for her limited ability while alive, but for the manner of her dying. I didn't think she deserved it. I didn't talk about this; just made a hard decision and got on with life. Then about six years later, one of my pupils, who bubbled over with the love of the Lord, assured me that 'Jesus would *get me* one day!' Quite uncharacteristically, I shared my anger at God with this child's mother, a virtual stranger to me at the time. I also spoke to her about my husband who had been unwell for many years, culminating in two huge operations – open-heart and abdominal. He lived with constant pain. She promised to pray for us both.

During November 1997 I became aware of hymns running through my head, good old-fashioned ones we'd sung at school. I told my husband and we thought perhaps I was becoming senile! But as they continued I came to accept them. They were just there. Sometimes I found myself singing them aloud. I told my praying friend. She was delighted, and pointed out that many of them were based on the psalms, so I was in fact receiving the word of God and praying! This continued into the new year and provided an inner refuge for me, as well as a talking point with my husband. Meanwhile, his health continued to deteriorate.

One day I found myself listening to a radio programme about a course called *Alpha*. Three days later my praying friend contacted me to say that she felt impelled to tell me about a course called *Alpha!* The upshot was that I began attending a course on the Hatty's farm at Norton. My husband showed an interest in how the course was going, and although he didn't always accept what I'd understood from one or other of the talks, we were able to discuss them. One discussion about forgiveness led to him letting go of a long-standing grudge, forgiving the person in question. This opened the way for us to begin to pray together. And for me it was time to realise the astonishing forgiveness that Jesus had made available to me through His dying on the cross and taking my sin.

After spells in and out of hospital towards the end of July my husband was re-admitted. I knew at last that I was facing a situation I had no control over. On 5 August he seemed to be a little better. At 10:30 a.m., as I was reading and praying, I knew we should pray a different prayer. He was awake and fully alert, and understood when I said that if he didn't want to say the words he was to say so. He smiled and agreed. We then prayed from Romans 10: 9, 10, 13: *"That if you confess with your mouth 'Jesus is Lord,' and believe in your heart that God raised Him from the dead, you will be saved. For it is with your heart that you believe and are justified, and it is with your mouth that you confess and are saved....Everyone who calls on the name of the Lord will be saved!"* I left at 4:30 p.m., to get home in daylight, and my beloved husband died at 5:30 p.m., safe, saved, and out of pain.

I went to our last *Alpha* session the next day, not a bit surprised to be there. I had to tell them about our prayers. In a way we were all elated. My *Alpha* story is not really one about pain, sickness, and death. It's a living testimony to the power and glory of God, through His Son our Lord Jesus Christ, and His Holy Spirit. It's also a down-to-earth, common-sense, acknowledgement of what an offence it is against God to try and control one's own life. Salvation is there for the asking.

Tiger Malleus.

Beryl Shaw

CHAPTER TWENTY

A Step in Faith

"But to each one is given the manifestation of the Spirit for the common good." 1 Corinthians 12: 7.

In my walk with the Lord I was continually reminded of the need to stay close to Him. I needed to be aware of His guidance and be sensitive to His voice. We never knew from one moment to the next how He was going to reveal Himself or what He might call us to do. The following story is an account of something that took many of us by surprise, especially me!

One evening a number of us had met together at the manse for a Bible Study. The minister led the study and we were greatly blessed by his profound knowledge, the study was insightful and very informative. Following a time of prayer together we then had a break for tea. Two or three of the ladies joined me in the kitchen and we busied ourselves with preparing the refreshments. While I was standing at a table one of the men walked through the kitchen, making his way to the back door. I turned to look at him and saw that he was holding his hand cupped, with the other hand underneath. I looked at him and said, "What have you got there Tom*?" he replied, "Ash," whereupon I replied, "Suss!" (It's an Afrikaans word expressing disgust.) Tom looked at me with a smile on his face, and, because we were talking, I followed him to the back door. I went down the steps, turned, and stood facing him in the doorway as he threw the ash outside. I continued speaking to him, saying, "That's a horrible habit Tom, in fact it should go!" With that I promptly addressed the spirit of nicotine. Initially I had been speaking to Tom in a light-hearted manner, but in that first split second of addressing the spirit, the thought that went through my mind, was, "This is not something I should be joking about, it's a serious business and should be dealt with accordingly." In that second I changed the tone of my voice and commanded the spirit of nicotine to come out of Tom immediately. Tom was taken by surprise and his face was the picture of amazement. We then had a short conversation before going through to the lounge for tea.

However, when I arrived home that evening it was with a certain sense of unease. I felt that I may have acted too hastily and in a way that was not acceptable to the Lord. I went before Him in prayer confessing my sin and telling Him how awful I felt. I was then led to pray, "But Lord, *if* You *did* do something in Tom's life and delivered him from that spirit, I ask that the next time he puts a cigarette to his mouth he will feel utterly sick and won't be able to smoke it!" The following morning I decided to go and speak to our minister and explain what had happened. As the leader of the church I felt that he should know that this had taken place. He was interested in what I had to say, and listened to me as I explained the details clearly. I told him that I thought I should also go around to Tom, explain myself and apologise to him also. He asked if I would like him to accompany me and I gladly accepted his offer.

Together we drove to the home where Tom and his wife, Sally*, invited us in to the familiar lounge. The minister sat reading a newspaper while I went through everything with our friends. I explained my years of involvement with the Inner Healing and Deliverance ministry and what led up to my actions of the previous evening. Tom and Sally listened in silence until I had finished. When I stopped talking Tom said, "Well, I'll tell you something, when I picked up a cigarette and put it to my mouth this morning it made me feel utterly sick! I couldn't smoke it." (I had not told Tom that this is what I had prayed the previous evening.) Our minister sat smiling to himself behind the newspaper and didn't say a word! Sally then went on to explain that Tom had been annoyed over what had taken place and had wanted to come around and see me. I do praise the Lord for Sally's calming influence on her husband as she encouraged him not to do anything in haste, but to wait, saying, "Beryl will explain it all to us." Praise God for loving, faithful friends with whom we can communicate in an atmosphere of love and acceptance. In the weeks that followed Tom remained in a state of amazement at what the Lord had done, (especially as he had tried, unsuccessfully, to give up smoking on several occasions previously). He often said to me, "You must do to Sally and Lesley*, (their daughter,) what you did to me!" I explained to him that, "It didn't quite work that way," but that my action was a "split-second prompting from the Lord in that given moment." I went on to say that, "We did not engineer our circumstances, but that they were God given opportunities for Him to display His power."

This took place in the mid 1990's and up until we left the country in 2004 Tom had not taken another cigarette. I praised God, not only for what he had accomplished in Tom's life, but also for the way that He undertook for me following my actions. Our friendships grew even stronger and God's name was glorified and uplifted through it all.

Incidents like these were an ongoing part of our daily lives and we lived in a state of perpetual wonder at what God was doing in our midst. We still lived with ongoing changes in the country and life held danger and difficulties. Yet we knew that God was with us and that we could turn to Him in any given moment.

During these years Mervyn and I were members of a prayer group comprising four married couples. This was a warm and loving group of gifted Christians. We met together on a regular basis for prayer and fellowship and the group was open to receive any who desired ministry, especially in the area of healing and deliverance. We were aware of the atrocities that were taking place around us, especially on the farms, and continual reports of harrowing stories were reported to us. Many of the families were known to us and these situations required constant prayer. We were also notified of God's amazing and miraculous interventions in the lives of people, which prompted evenings of praise and worship to our mighty God. It was a privilege and a blessing to meet with this group of Christians. Faith was at its highest level and the gifts amongst us flowed in unison. Time and time again we were faced with "humanly impossible" situations in the lives of people who came for ministry. We praised God for His presence and power among us. It was with great joy and thanksgiving that we celebrated the Lord's goodness as He touched lives, and set people free from bondages that had held them for years.

CHAPTER TWENTY ONE

Abiding Under His Shadow

"For He will give His angels charge concerning you, to guard you in all your ways." Psalm 91: 11

Although we were surrounded by violence of every kind, it has not been my intention to expound upon the negative and destructive forces that were at work within the country. The world is only too aware of the tragedies and violence that have taken place in Zimbabwe, as with many other countries. My aim, rather, has been to centre in upon what God was doing in and around us in the midst of the difficulties and tragedies. As a result of His amazing presence with us I feel the need to share what He has done in our lives, and in the words of Peter I say, *"for we cannot stop speaking what we have seen and heard."* (ACTS 4: 20)

God's hand of protection was upon us in so many different ways. It was not unusual to find ourselves in frightening circumstances, which were beyond our control; but God's strength and presence was always there. Miraculously, attacks were averted in the most unexpected ways. On numerous occasions the Lord intervened in what would, or could, have been a potentially nasty assault upon ourselves or our friends, and He protected us.

The following testimony is just one of many such incidences.

My Testimony
Robbie Saunders

Aug/Sept 1995 ...I was parked on the edge of a road, in a residential area, two houses up from where Debs, our daughter was having lessons.

Across the road (in a cul de sac) on the driver's side of my vehicle, in full view, were two ladies having tea in their lounge, with the windows open; and on the passenger side of my vehicle, behind an open wire fence, a gardener was working. No-one heard or saw a thing. ONLY Debs heard the hooter and my loud noises and knew I was in trouble. This is what happened...

Whilst sitting inside the two-door station wagon reading, I observed an orange Peugeot sedan drive past me. THEN I heard this voice say "lock the door from which Debbie has alighted." Immediately I did so and turned to lock my driver's door only to be confronted by a man, holding his hands to his face, who said "DON'T MAKE A NOISE." He kept looking past me to the passenger door.

A very calm thought entered my mind. I was safe from any intrusion from that area as I had locked the door; concentrate on taking in all his details and HOOT and make a noise - scream This I did without panic.

His hand went over my mouth, another calm thought came to me - bite hard which I did. His hand was removed and the car door whipped open. He literally took me by the scruff of my neck and yanked me out, and threw me onto the tarmac. He had two accomplices, one of whom put his knees on my shoulders from behind with his hands around my throat choking me. The other promptly put his thighs onto my thighs. Another calm thought... you are going to be raped... tell them to just take the car...

Without hesitation I calmly said, "Why don't you just take the car." Suddenly they were in the car, and had started it. Another thought... my shoes were in the car under the driver's seat and it was going to be a long walk without them. I thrust my head into the driver's window and shouted "Give me back my shoes; they are the only pair I have." The driver, shocked, shouted back at me, "Where are they?" "Under the seat," I retorted. My shoes were thrown out and off they went.

I walked back to where Debs was and calmed the lady of the house who had witnessed the incident. We prayed, giving thanks to the Lord Jesus for my protection and safety. Then I phoned the company who owned the car. The safe and office keys and a blank signed company cheque were in my bag in the car. Then I phoned the police, and finally my precious husband, who stopped a police car and brought them along.

Only God, My Father's protection saved me from harm and panic.

Robbie Saunders.

....

When Robbie phoned to tell me of this incident, she was adamant that we did not centre our thoughts upon the negative aspect of what had happened, but that we praise the Lord for His intervention and protection upon her life. Also for the fact that throughout the ordeal she had not experienced any fear. We certainly recognised that God had been with her and had imparted His peace and courage. We were so grateful that our friend had been left unharmed. We also saw the amusing side in that Robbie had the courage and presence of mind to shout after the men and demand her shoes!

In so many instances it was clearly evident that when a person stood upon God's promises, he was given remarkable strength to stand against the attacks of the evil one. Time and time again we saw the name of Jesus Christ being uplifted and glorified in the most dreadful, (and often *unusual,*) circumstances, as evidenced in the following story.

Mervyn and I were members of a Christian Library by the name of "Manna Books and Tapes." The library was owned and run by a friend, Mary*, and was situated in Avondale, a suburb of Harare. One Saturday morning as we entered the library we were greeted by a very excited Mary. She immediately asked us if we had just seen a particular lady. We did not know the person she had named, but I will call her Joan. Mary then went on to tell us that Joan had left the library only a short while before us and had related the following incident. Having left the library she walked to the area where she had parked her car, but was just in time to see it disappearing down the road, approximately 100 metres away. Whereupon Joan immediately ran to the centre of the very busy main road, pointed her hand in the direction of the rapidly departing car and shouted very loudly, *"In the name of Jesus, STOP!"* With that the car came to a sudden halt, all the doors were flung open and the occupants of the car simply abandoned the vehicle and fled! Joan then went to retrieve her car and returned to the library to relay the account to Mary.

On another occasion Mary herself was subjected to an assault. She had just left the library and was walking towards her nearby home when suddenly her shoulder-bag slipped from her shoulder and fell to the ground. Being aware of incidents like this she stopped abruptly, realising that the leather strap had been sliced through with a knife and that the person, or persons, behind her, were intent on robbing, or harming her. In relating the incident to me at a later stage Mary explained that she had been concerned that the men, (it turned out to be two,) would steal the keys to the library or her home. She was more concerned about the former. I cannot recall her exact words to the men, but I do remember her saying that "The Lord gave her words of wisdom in dealing with them." The men were angry and displayed a threatening attitude towards Mary, but in a most remarkable way, and with great courage, she steered the conversation with them right away from the contents of her bag, particularly the keys. With the result being that they not only left her alone, and unharmed, but they also disregarded the keys altogether. What amazing strength and peace of mind the Lord imparts to us when we place ourselves confidently and trustingly in His protective hands.

As I remember the following incident, I often shake my head when I think of the naïve ways I have trusted people throughout my life. Nevertheless, the fact of the Lord's protection upon me has been brought home to me in an undeniable way, as evidenced in the following account.

Early one morning I was standing at the sink washing the breakfast dishes. The family had left for work and school and I was alone in the house. I became aware that someone was banging on our front gates, so I left the dishes and made my way down the long front garden. A black African was standing outside. He explained that he had just come from the church where he had requested help and the minister had helped him to the best of his ability. In response to my enquiry the man told me the following story. He had travelled from Bulawayo and had arrived at the

Harare railway station that morning. On his arrival he was robbed of all his money and possessions. His young son had just died and he had not yet had time to bury him. Feeling extremely sorry for him, I unlocked the gate and invited him in to the house. I asked him if he had eaten anything that morning, whereupon he told me that he had not, so I made him some porridge. While he was eating he went on to tell me that he was a school teacher in Bulawayo and gave me the name of the school. He asked if he could use the telephone to phone the school and I gave him my permission. I then proceeded to phone other churches in an effort to raise funds for him. I was not successful in this because their policy was to offer practical help, but not monetary. I explained to him that I did not keep much money in the house and that I only had a little change, which I offered to him. He declined to take it. I did consider walking down to the post office with him, which was about a mile and a half away, to withdraw some money for him, but, for various reasons, decided against the idea. He was in the house for just under an hour. After he had used the bathroom I walked down to the gate with him and he left. He returned about half an hour later to ask whether I had found any more money yet. I explained that I hadn't, but that he was welcome to the change I had. Once again he declined to take it.

The following day I was speaking to some of the Shona ladies in our congregation, I told them of this incident. As my story unfolded their faces displayed looks of disbelief. They could not believe that I had actually invited this man into our home. They explained that he was a local, well-known con-man and that their children had strict instructions not to allow him even through the gate of their property. They said that he was a very dangerous man and were horrified when I told them that he was carrying a briefcase. They said that it was likely that he either had a gun or a knife in the case. Under our circumstances in the country this was very probable. They also added that "God must have been with you and was protecting you," and "that you are very lucky to be alive."

It turned out that there was no school in Bulawayo known by the name that the man had given me, and that he had not actually made any phone calls in my presence. He had simply been speaking into an unconnected line. Following this incident I realised that I had acted very unwisely by inviting a stranger into our home while I was alone, and as a result I became deeply aware of God's hand of protection upon my life on this occasion.

Another example of God's protecting hand occurred when Mervyn and I were travelling through a housing area that was known for its unrest and crime. We were on our way to visit our family and were sitting at a road junction waiting for the traffic lights to turn to green, so that we could proceed. Mervyn was driving. Suddenly, with no warning, the driver's door was pulled open and two men peered into the car. We were completely taken by surprise and Mervyn shouted at the man and told him to go away (words to that effect!). Whereupon the two men stepped back and simply said, "Oh sorry, sorry!" the lights changed and we continued on our way.

We were used to hearing of incidents where people had been dragged from their vehicles and severely assaulted, so we were very well aware that once again the Lord had intervened and miraculously protected us.

Yet another incident that revealed God's hand of protection upon us took place during the night when we were sleeping. Burglaries were the "norm" in most homes so people slept under lock and key. Homes were fitted with alarms and security devices of every kind and interior doors were locked when sleeping. We had already experienced several burglaries, so we secured our home to the best of our ability and retired to bed. However, I was a little concerned that we did not have a key to one particular door and therefore could not lock it. The door was an important one because it was the door that separated the bedrooms from the living area. As we could not lock it we took other precautions and piled numerous items against the door every night (including a bell, known as "Grannies bell!"), the idea being that in the event of intruders we would at least have some warning of their presence.

We slept peacefully through the night, but when I woke the next morning and walked first through the kitchen, (where our two large dogs were still sleeping peacefully,) and then through the dining room, I became distinctly uneasy. I opened the door to the lounge and was shocked at what I saw. The curtains and French doors on my right were still closed and undisturbed, but the two sets of windows facing me on the opposite side of the room had been severely damaged. The windows had been broken and glass was strewn over the carpet, the burglar bars (all homes were automatically fitted with these on construction) had been cut through at the base and bent up, leaving a gap large enough for a person to enter. The curtains had also been wound up and threaded through the top of the bars. I then noticed that our complete sound system, along with all tapes and CDs had been taken, plus photographs and several other items. We were particularly distressed over a special photo of our daughter, one that had been taken in England and could not be replaced at the time. We were also sad at loosing the frame as this had been a gift from a dear friend.

Initially we could not understand why the house alarm had not sounded and why neither we, nor the dogs, had been undisturbed and had not heard a single sound. As far as the alarm was concerned we eventually came to realise that the intruders had, amazingly, somehow avoided the security beam, which resulted in the alarm not sounding. However, several people still questioned the fact that we had not heard anything, also, especially questioning why the dogs had not barked. At that time, in an effort to gain access to properties, burglars had taken to using an ether spray to put the occupants of homes to sleep. When doing a thorough search around our bedroom windows we discovered that a log of wood had been placed beneath the high windows and clear signs of finger prints were imprinted on the burglar bars. The bedroom windows had been open, as with the kitchen windows. We then came to realise why we and the dogs had not been disturbed. We had been very effectively put to sleep!

Other experiences like this left us with a feeling of vulnerability. It was also disturbing to know that one's privacy had been invaded. However, I praised the Lord that in actual fact we *had* been asleep, because if we had woken up and gone to investigate there is absolutely no telling what may have happened to us. I was truly grateful that the Lord had been watching over us and had brought us safely through this, (and many other) nights.

Unfortunately by this stage in the country's life the insurance companies had almost collapsed and claims were taking many years to be settled, if they ever were. As a result we received no compensation for this loss.

Shortly before our departure from the country I came to realise with a far deeper understanding the numerous occasions when the Lord had surrounded us with His guardian angels. For many years the city centre had not been a safe place to go, but our imminent emigration from the country necessitated visiting the area. While Mervyn went into various offices I remained outside. I was on my own sitting in a locked car, with a book for company. At the time I was not in the least bit afraid and thought little about the fact that I was a lone woman. A locked car was little deterrent to any person with intent to harm. However, I was never disturbed by anyone in any way. Once again, with hindsight, I realised just how immense God's love and protection was upon us and we give Him all thanks and praise.

CHAPTER TWENTY TWO

His Plan Prevails

"Do not fear, for I am with you; do not anxiously look about you, for I am your God. I will strengthen you, surely I will help you, surely I will uphold you with My righteous right hand."
Isaiah 41: 10.

From Philippians 1: verse 6 , *"For I am confident of this very thing, that He who began a good work in you will perfect it until the day of Christ Jesus."*

Once again I became extremely aware of the truth of these words through the following episode. I was reminded, yet again, that God does not leave His work unfinished in our lives, no matter how frightening or severe the circumstances may be.

I recall one particular Saturday evening in 2000. I was working at the dining room table preparing the music for the worship service the following morning, when I became aware that Mervyn had been coughing continuously for ages. Eventually he asked me if I would take him in to the Trauma Centre as he was having difficulty in breathing. Mervyn has never been in the habit of making a fuss about anything and appeared quite calm. I had virtually finished the preparation of the music, so I was able to stop at that point. I put everything together and asked him if, on our way, we could call around at the church and leave the music there. (My intention was to leave a note with the music, asking Sue to take over from me in the morning if necessary.) He agreed. It took a while to lock the house up, set the house alarm and unlock the gates to the carport. Eventually we were ready to leave and I climbed into the driver's seat of the car. Most vehicles in the country were fitted with security devices as a deterrent against theft, so I searched under the dashboard for the cut-out switch. Try as I might I could not locate it. I was always in the habit of driving any of our vehicles, but this was a new company vehicle which I had not yet had chance to use.

With his laboured breathing Mervyn told me to drive down to the gate, (some distance away from the house,) and once there have another look for the switch. At the gate I climbed out of the car to unlock the padlock. (Our home was surrounded by a 7-foot wall with glass on the top of it. The high gates were of solid metal.) I then drove the car through the gates, got out and re-locked them, and then continued hunting for the cut-out switch. It was nowhere to be found! With great difficulty Mervyn climbed out of the car and came around to the driver's side to look for the cut-out himself. Unfortunately he couldn't locate it either. Eventually he disconnected the wiring under the bonnet. He stood beside the car without moving for what seemed ages while I urged him to get into the car. Breathing was now very difficult for him, but eventually he climbed in. Once having delivered the music to the church I then drove as quickly as I dared to the Trauma Centre. It was only a six mile journey but traffic conditions were often problematic. With constant power cuts the traffic lights were unserviceable more often than not. Accidents and traffic jams were the norm and one had to stay alert when driving.

Eventually we arrived at the Centre and on seeing Mervyn's condition a nurse quickly brought a wheelchair. He was immediately taken to be X-rayed. On returning, the nurse asked if he, "Had always had a heart condition?" We told her that we had never been aware of any heart condition. The doctor on duty came and questioned me, (he addressed me very sharply). As he viewed the X-rays of Mervyn's heart he just stood shaking his head. He informed us that the heart was double its size and Mervyn's blood sugar level was over 20 mmol/l (Up to 10 mmol/l would have been acceptable!). Mervyn was then taken to a ward and I notified the family. Within half an hour they had arrived as they all lived locally.

The Trauma Centres are designed for emergencies only. Patients are generally treated and then, if necessary, sent to a hospital. Mervyn's condition was so grave that it would have been dangerous to move him farther. He was suffering heart failure and needed immediate attention. We were also facing a further problem in that we had recently applied for new medical insurance cards, which had not yet arrived. (We were covered for medical insurance, but did not have the cards to prove it, and as it was a weekend the centre were unable to phone to confirm it.) The hospital would not accept a patient without proof of medical insurance cover or payment of an admission fee of $59,000. The Trauma Centre required $20,000. This we did not have, but the family offered to cover the sum required between them. Meanwhile the doctor proceeded to attend to Mervyn and he was kept at the Trauma Centre overnight. The family left, but I remained by his bedside praying hour by hour through the night. Miraculously the Lord sustained his life through the prompt and efficient attention of the doctor.

The following morning another doctor was on duty and he gave permission for Mervyn's discharge. Unfortunately his condition deteriorated through the day and I drove him back to the Trauma Centre that evening. Once again the original doctor was on duty and it was evident by his manner that he was very annoyed that Mervyn had been discharged. He again informed us that Mervyn's condition was critical and once again admitted him to the centre where he spent a second night. I returned home intending to return early the following morning, at which time I was to meet the cardiologist.

The following morning, as I opened the gates to drive the car through, a very upsetting thing happened. As quick as lightening one of our dogs (Chantie) ran out on to the road and ran right in front of an oncoming car. I actually saw her body bowl under the vehicle and roll out into the ditch on the other side of the road. I ran out to her, expecting to see her severely hurt, but to my amazement she bounced back up and ran to me. I took her back into the house and phoned a friend. I explained that I was in a hurry as I was on the way to see Mervyn, and asked if one of their family could come and check Chantie for any injuries that I may have missed. Incredibly our little dog appeared to be unhurt, but I was concerned about just leaving her after experiencing such a fright. Once again I praise the Lord for special friends. Their daughter agreed to come around and check her over, which she did soon after I had left. She found Chantie in high spirits and could see no obvious injury. We were so grateful to the Lord for protecting her as she was a very special little dog to us.

Unfortunately as a result of this incident I arrived at the centre later than intended and missed seeing the cardiologist. However I spoke to the doctor who informed me that Mervyn's condition had improved and that he would be transferred to a hospital that morning. We had great admiration for this doctor and praised the Lord for his dedication and medical skill. We later learnt that he was a very highly qualified cardiac surgeon and was of Russian nationality.

It was with relief that our medical insurance cards arrived on the Monday morning and Mervyn was transferred to a hospital without delay. It was discovered at this time that he was diabetic and was immediately prescribed a high dosage of insulin. He remained in the hospital for less than a week, during which time his condition was stabilised.

During the course of the following year Mervyn had regular appointments with the cardiologist. (By this time we had learnt that he was one of only two cardiologists in the country. He was also very highly qualified and his services were in great demand. He not only practiced in Zimbabwe, but also in Nigeria and Tanzania.) As the months went by the specialist was astounded over the speedy recovery that Mervyn was making. Within one year Mervyn's heart had returned to its normal size, and, with the correct diet, his blood sugar levels had dropped from more than 20 mmol/l to about 6 or 7 mmol/l, and the level of insulin was reduced from 80 units to 40 per day. We recognised God's hand in raising up the medical people who had attended Mervyn throughout this time, and also the incredible recovery that had taken place in only 12 months.

Mervyn remained in good health until four years later when he suffered a heart attack. He had been admitted to hospital where he was undergoing a small prostate operation. It was just six weeks before we were due to emigrate. I had taken him to the hospital and had returned home. During the course of the morning I received a phone call from the surgeon who had just performed the surgery. He said, (in a quiet, calm voice,) "Mrs Shaw, could you come into the hospital and see me. I had got about three quarters of the way through the operation, when I think your husband had a heart attack." (This was later confirmed.) I immediately contacted the family and then drove to the hospital. For the next two days Mervyn's condition was critical. Thereafter he started to recover. Once again the Lord had miraculously intervened and pulled him through and the operation had been a success. He should have been in hospital for approximately three days, but unfortunately caught a hospital infection and remained in there for two weeks. The heart attack was attributed to the high levels of stress under which he had been working.

Six weeks before we were due to fly, our home was sold, and, after 31 years of family life there, we moved out. We praise God for our family who opened their home to us for the remainder of our stay in the country. We enjoyed a most comfortable arrangement with them while we dealt with last-minute arrangements. I also praise the Lord for our son-in-law, who coped speedily and efficiently one evening when Mervyn suffered a bad reaction from the lingering infection.

During the course of the next four weeks a great deal of effort on the part of our family was put into locating the prescribed medicine to combat the infection. Unfortunately the drug was unobtainable in Zimbabwe and was eventually sent up from S.A. Mervyn returned to hospital for a week as the drug had to be administered intravenously. To our disappointment the results were only partially successful.

There is no doubt whatsoever that the Lord carried us through the last few weeks in the country. Underneath were the everlasting arms. Only He could have imparted the strength that was required to cope with the ongoing demands. Apart from Mervyn's ill health and the legalities connected with our emigration, we were also coping with the sale of our home. On one occasion Mervyn was required to sign an important document in connection with his settlement visa. We drove the 10 miles to the agency, only to discover that he was too weak to climb the flight of stairs up to the office. The appointment was abandoned and we had to wait until he had regained his strength before we could return.

With only three weeks to go before our departure it was imperative that Mervyn's heart condition was stabilised. Once again he attended the cardiologist and once again God showed Himself to be a mighty God. Mervyn's medical condition, and the circumstances in which we found ourselves, were almost a repeat of those of four years previously. The speed with which the Lord brought healing to his body had to be seen to be believed. So much so, that on one occasion the cardiologist could not believe, (or accept) the readings of an E.C.G., which had been sent to him from the medical centre. He repeated the tests there and then himself, and found the results to be identical to those he already had before him.

Everyone was praying for Mervyn's speedy recovery. Understandably the specialist could not give permission for him to fly until he was satisfied with his health. As the date of our planned departure drew closer the cardiologist was amazed at how quickly the test results were coming back to normal. Even we, with our limited knowledge, were astounded over the dramatic improvement that was taking place before our eyes. There could be no other explanation for this miracle of healing, other than the hand of God.

With just a few days remaining before our departure date the cardiologist was satisfied with the results and agreed to sign a discharge certificate.

We were free to fly!

Now to Him who is able to do exceeding abundantly beyond all that we ask or think, according to the power that works within us, to Him be the glory in the church and in Christ Jesus to all generations forever and ever. Amen.
Ephesians 3: 20.

For more information contact:

Beryl Shaw
C/O Advantage Books
P.O. Box 160847
Altamonte Springs, FL 32716

info@ advbooks.com

To purchase additional copies of this book or other books published by
Advantage Books call our order number at:

407-788-3110 (Book Orders Only)

or visit our bookstore website at:
www.advbookstore.com

Longwood, Florida, USA
"we bring dreams to life"™
www.advbooks.com

Lightning Source UK Ltd.
Milton Keynes UK
UKOW05f0332021216
289050UK00019B/905/P